REELLY

Unbelievable Fly Fishing Guide Stories

Ryan Johnston

Cover image by DeYoung Studio

Book design by Anna Burrous

ISBN 978-1-7372556-1-1

First Edition: March 2024

DEDICATION

I will always dedicate every book, first and foremost, to my beautiful, intelligent, and loving wife, Bonnie. I am so fortunate that we found each other in college. Thank you for being supportive of me and for loving our family so well. You are the glue that keeps us all together. I can't imagine doing life with anyone else. We make a great team, and I look forward to having you by my side for the rest of my life. I love you, my bride.

To my two girls, you are the greatest gift God has ever given me. I am so fortunate to be your dad. You have taught me so much – how to love deeper, and to find even greater appreciation through your eyes, your perspectives. You are great teachers! As you go through life, there will be hard times. Hard times can still be good. Soak up the good times; enjoy every minute you can. Weather the storm during the hard times, knowing that God is always for you and with you, and your family too. You can accomplish great things if you work hard and surround yourselves with good people. A good life requires a strong, loving tribe surrounding and supporting you. Your mom and I will always be in your tribe, cheering you on.

And finally, I dedicate this book to all the readers of my first book, *A Reel Job*. I wrote it entirely for the love of the creative process of writing stories. I love a good story. But I never imagined publishing a second book. I did continue to write stories as I experienced them, just for the joy of the process. Many readers sent private messages, sharing with me how much they enjoyed the book; some were friends, and some were complete strangers! I'm still shocked so many of you enjoyed it – who would have thought a fly fishing guide who always struggled with school writing assignments could write and publish a book people would enjoy?! *Not me!* Many asked, "Will you write another one? When's the next one?" Thank you for your generous spirits, your kindness, encouragement, and support. Because of your feedback, I decided to publish a sequel. I hope you find as much laughter, joy, and connection as with the first. I am humbled by your purchase, the very real way it supports my family, and the joy it brings me to bring you something you enjoy. I'm just grateful for it all.

And to every reader; past, present, or future: cheers to pursuing your passions in the great outdoors! If you find yourself in Montana, I'd love to take you fly fishing. Who knows, maybe you'll make the third book. I promise I won't use your real name!

TABLE OF CONTENTS

PROLOGUE

To be honest, I'm not a huge reader. I'd rather be fishing. When I do read, I've found I really like to know whose writing I'm reading. Understanding the author enhances my understanding of the writing, and adds to my enjoyment.

My first book, *A Reel Job*, gives a glimpse into my personal life and history, my sense of humor, and my appreciation for connecting with people and their stories. Now here's a more cohesive take on this author; I hope it deepens your reading experience.

My absolute favorite part of life is people. I love hanging out with people. Not a lot of people, though. I am a complete introvert. I prefer smaller groups of 4 to 6 people at a time. At a large party, you will find me in the corner enjoying a cocktail and observing the room. Because honestly, I prefer the deeper conversations that happen in smaller groups.

I love having fun. Who doesn't? Scoring a 7 on the Enneagram a few years ago was an interesting aha moment. Of course, it's not a perfect test- what is? But it has brought me greater understanding and insights into my tendencies. Sevens are nicknamed "Enthusiasts," generally motivated by a desire to be happy. Sevens like to plan enjoyable activities, contribute to the world, and introduce others to new experiences and adventures.

Man, does that description fit me well. I love adventures. More than that, I love sharing adventures with others, which is probably the reason I guide, and definitely the reason I decided to write a second book. I believe these stories have value and they're worth sharing; they give us insights into our interactions, they encourage and celebrate connection with the natural world, and they bring us to laughter and reflection.

Now onto life's pillars. How about a super-fast snapshot of my life?

Believe in Jesus. Saved by grace. Only child. Parents still married. Grew up in San Diego. Started fishing at age 4, fly fishing at age 12. Moved north for college. Met my wife freshman year in the dorms. Happily married to my best friend since 2006; our adventures never let up. Started guiding professionally in college. UC Davis business degree. Immediately moved north again for grad school. CSU Chico MBA. During grad school, inspired by a sermon at church and an awesome day on the river with a boy and his uncle, I started a nonprofit called Cast Hope to give the gift of fly fishing to underserved, at-risk kids. Then came two beautiful, sweet, funny, full of wonder daughters. Published my first book, *A Reel Job,* in 2021. Moved to Northwest Montana in 2022. Still Executive Director of Cast Hope, with four current regions and more in the future, God willing. Still guiding, still writing.

What about the fishing pillars? I prefer saltwater fishing over freshwater fishing, though I guide in the freshwater. That doesn't make sense?! The only freshwater fishing I absolutely love is coastal steelheading. Coastal steelheading is an addiction, and I'm currently dealing with significant withdrawals. I prefer to fish in tropical climates over cold climates. That's a problem when it comes to steelheading in the rain! Fishing the flats is my absolute favorite. Fishing offshore pelagic species would be a close second. I like hooking big fish that pull hard and rip off a ton of line.

How about other random facts? I used to be a diehard San Diego Chargers fan. *Not* a Los Angeles Chargers fan. Now a bitter NFL football fan. Love fantasy football. Love watching any sports. Go Padres. Favorite shoes are flip flops. Favorite place is on the beach. Love watching live music. Love Broadway—*Hamilton, Les Misérables, Phantom,* and *Rent.* Fascinated by science. Love scotch. Love red wine. Love a gin and tonic. Love an old fashioned. Love margaritas. Love good tequila. Love IPAs. Is that too many drinks? Never.

Well, now you've got the snapshot, and I hope you are entertained by the book even more. This is a collection of awesome, unbelievable but true stories from the water, names changed, of course. Enjoy the perspectives, the journey, the adventure, and of course, the laughs. *Cheers!*

DON'T QUIT YOUR DAY JOB

Every fishing guide in the world has been told how amazing our "office" is.

It's true: Profound natural beauty fills our workplace. We are blessed. Looking for the next great fishing spot on an emerald-green steelhead river, a cold, clear mountain stream, or the turquoise blue flats is truly magical. Most clients feel a sense of envy as they bask in the wonder of these wild places – the places they go on their "days off."

"Man, you know how lucky you are to be out here? You're not sitting behind a desk or stuck in a cubicle. Most days I just pine for a glimpse of daylight!"

It's true, humans were made to be outside more than they are these days. So most guides nod our heads in agreement, acknowledging that we get to work in amazing places.

However, most of us don't tell you, your office sounds pretty damn nice some days.

I always hate to rain on a parade. But in reality, guiding is not as sexy as many make it out to be (guides included). The hours are long, the job is harsh, and the "office" is very temperamental. Guides live for the days when there is no wind, the tides and river flows are perfect, and there are hungry fish everywhere.

Those days are few and far between.

More often than not, the wind does blow, the water conditions are not great, and the fish are picky little bitches. We all try our best to make our clients' days on the water as enjoyable as possible, but there are so many variables outside our control. Most of them, actually.

When the weather decides to give us a punch in the gut, we long for that nice, warm cubicle. When the wind is blowing straight in our faces at 30 miles an hour, and we're using every last fiber of every muscle to row you down the river, we *may* not be having fun. When the tide is ripping, and we have to pole across the flat, rest assured there will be icing of sore muscles that night. Our hands hurt, our backs are sore, and we're trying our best to overcome the obstacles. The windows of your office look kinda nice on those gusty days.

On the big rainy days, staying dry evades us. There's nothing we can do. Sure, we all have really nice rain gear from Simms, Patagonia, or Marmot. No knocks against them; they make some real fine gear. And in a steady rainstorm, there is no gear in the world that will keep us completely dry. A thunderstorm rolls in…temperatures begin to drop…hail bullets of all sizes pelt our heads, arms, legs, feet. No gear protects us from that.

I'm no gladiator, and I don't pretend to be one; every time, I long for the safety of your office roof.

Guides in the mountains must constantly deal with freezing temperatures. As rain turns to snow, fingertips burn and sting and fumble. We blow into our curled hands to get the blood flowing again. We're dreaming about jumping into that hot shower when we get home. The heater in your nice, warm office sounds really good on those bitterly cold days.

Guides in the tropics deal with oppressive heat and humidity. Their clothes are always sticking to their bodies. Sweat constantly rolls down their faces and backs, and their bodies struggle to retain enough fluids to stay hydrated. Every guide's worst nightmare is uncontrollable, dehydrated muscle cramps as we try to row or pole a boat.

But don't get me wrong. These wild places are magical.

One sweltering summer day, I was guiding in Redding, California, and the temperature hit 118 degrees. I'm a numbers guy, and by my humble calculations, I drank more than 250 fluid ounces of Gatorade and water. The crazy thing is, not once did I have to pee. The sweating was enough. Truly every ounce of liquid I consumed that day leaked out through my pores. Later that evening, I had one of the worst headaches of my life due to the temperature in my "beautiful office."

So the normal office setting, even with all its very real limitations and annoyances, does come with some perks. The temperature-controlled rooms, the protection from the elements, the air quality filtered free of wildfire smoke particles and agricultural sprays, and the generally violence-free environment are all attributes that workday folks tend to take for granted. Heck, restrooms are a nice perk too. As guides, we know we work in beautiful places, we enjoy a lot of freedom on the job, and supervisors aren't constantly looking over our shoulders (just clients- ha!). We also recognize that our jobs have some major limitations.

One of the biggest concerns for all guides is exposure to the sun. Whether it's guiding for trout in the Rockies, Atlantic salmon in Norway, giant trevally in the Seychelles, or permit on the flats of Florida, one major concern is skin cancer. We can buy sunscreen in bulk and apply it all day long, use all kinds of protective gear, but still we incur nasty sunburns and weird tan lines.

Having guided many, many years in the year-round California sun, I used to wonder if my two young daughters would even recognize me without my raccoon eye tan. When I look at myself in the mirror, I wonder how long until I get the first skin cancer removed from my face. Sometimes, I wonder if my wife is truly gazing at my handsome mug or just examining me for suspicious splotches. In those moments, I think, "What am I doing?" I do admit, I wonder what it's like, sitting in that nice office. "Is it all that bad?"

Enough about the extreme conditions guides endure while working in the "best office in the world." I can't leave out what happens to our bodies—how our shoulders, wrists, elbows, and backs get worn out little by little from the repetitive, hard work of moving boats around.

Or how calluses grow like mini mountains on our hands from rowing or poling the boat to the next fishing spot.

Or how our feet are constantly cracked from getting in and out of water all day, or how handling fish so frequently takes the natural oils out of our hands and makes the skin crackle and peel. Or all the times a wayward fish hook embeds itself in our flesh (which are many). There are a lot of things our clients don't consider when they think about us getting paid to fish.

Oh, and allow me to clarify something: *Guides do not fish for a living*. Funny how much we hear that, though. To be honest, most of our clients fish more than we do. Yes, we take people fishing for a living. But when was the last time you saw a guide reel in a fish?

Now don't get your panties in a twist. That doesn't mean we don't *love* helping our clients catch fish. We really, really love it. We take GREAT satisfaction in knowing we were a large part of that last fish you landed. We even love being out there. At the end of the day, though, this is a profession with a high number of risks, including skin cancer, broken down bodies, extreme environmental exposure, and having to deal with clients' sometimes dramatic mood swings. Did I mention the mood swings?

I would hate to make you think guiding is misery. Just giving you the full perspective. Let me leave you with a funny story about one of my worst moments from 20 years of guiding. It's an experience I hope I never have to relive ... and one that will forever make me laugh.

Picture this: perfect weather, beautiful spring day, the Feather River, Northern California. My clients, Rob and Steve, were all about the spring steelhead. It was one of those days when all you corporate guys feel especially jealous of our office. The sky was clear and bluebird, with a few beautiful white clouds. We had a great first half of our day, with five beautiful chromed-out steelhead brought to the net. All of the fish were in that 4- to 6-pound class, in great shape—nice, bright, silver fish.

A few minutes after lunch, Rob hooked another fish, which instantly rocketed upriver and then hunkered down on the bottom. After about 20 seconds, I knew Rob didn't have a steelhead on his line.

"I think you hooked a sucker fish, Rob," I said.

He looked back at me, face fallen with disappointment, and nodded in agreement. After a few more minutes of fighting, we finally got a glimpse of the brown and yellow fish swimming on the bottom of the river. Suck.

Rob eventually landed the sucker. Pulling it out of the net, I noticed Rob's fly had snagged the fish in the stomach. Suck again. I carefully, firmly, held the fish behind its two pectoral fins and turned its stomach toward me to get the hook out of its belly. As I struggled to mercifully free the fish from the fly, the fish thanked me by shaking hard and shooting a stream of white "gunk" onto my face!

A fire hose of baby fish juice sprayed all over my sunglasses, beard, and mouth. That's right. I said mouth.

Instantly, I turned my face away as the money shot continued, coating my sideburns and ear. I couldn't drop the fish for fear of the second hook burying into my hand. I yelled out in disgust as I pulled back, shaking my head back and forth. Was this really happening?! Sticky goo dripped from my sunglasses as I lowered my head.

In the haste of a combat medic, I got the hook out and threw that nasty fish back in the water. I thumped back into my seat and took a moment, in shock from the ordeal. SUCK!

Within seconds, Rob and Steve broke into uproarious laughter. Their guide had been slimed with…fish ejaculate.

A sink and some soap would have been nice. Trying to get clean and get back to work, I proceeded to pour bottle after bottle of water on my face. Lots of scrubbing and little by little, the fish mess washed away. I felt deeply grateful that my mouth was closed when the sucker spewed. After about 10 minutes of washing myself and gagging back vomit, we got back to fishing. Rob and Steve caught a handful more steelhead, but the highlight of their day, no doubt, was witnessing their guide get blasted in the face.

Think about that the next time you wanna quit your day job and "fish for a living" in the great outdoors.

PERSPECTIVE

The one place in this world almost all anglers dream about is Alaska. Home of wild salmon, beautiful steelhead, pumpkin-orange arctic char, and monster rainbows. Whether your passion is swinging for chromers, chasing cohos, or fishing mice for aggressive leopard rainbow trout, most anglers either dream of their first trip to the Last Frontier, or they're mentally planning their next one.

However, once you've fished Alaska a handful of times, it starts to change your perspective on the rest of your fishing. When Alaska becomes your baseline, it's pretty difficult for local fishing trips to compare. The Alaska-skewed brain thinks about trout in pounds rather than in inches. Those once-beautiful and impressive 16-inch trout from your local watershed don't have quite the same appeal. Thank you, Alaska.

One of my best friends guided at a high-end, fly-out lodge in Alaska for 5 summers, and his guiding and fishing experiences there absolutely ruined him. When you get used to catching 25- to 30-inch rainbows, coming home and fishing for "normal-sized" trout doesn't really move the excitement meter. My friend would ultimately stop fishing for trout in the Lower 48 altogether, shifting his attention to steelhead out of a need to pursue something more powerful and more challenging to catch.

When I guided in Northern California, every fall my clients would come out and tell of great adventures on their summer trips to Alaska. Over time, due to their frequent Alaska fishing, their perspectives and fishing expectations became...clouded.

I once had the privilege of guiding an NBA Hall of Famer I'll call Ben to avoid a possible lawsuit. Ben had always wanted to fish for striped bass, so he scheduled a summer trip with me on the Sacramento River. The thought of having a famous athlete in the boat was exciting to me. I looked forward to stories of players I had watched and idolized as a kid. It was the first time I had ever guided a famous athlete, and the best part was that Ben had fished all over the world. And what do you know, Alaska was his absolute favorite.

I met Ben at the boat launch. We made small talk about the teams he had played for and his perspective on the game while I prepped the boat. As I listened to his stories about the golden days, I rigged up our fly rods for the mission of catching Ben his first striper.

To catch stripers on the Sac, we cast shooting-head fly lines, a type of fly line made to sink. Each one has a different sink rate: some slower, others faster. Generally, the more weight built into a line, the faster it sinks—and the more difficult it is to cast. If you've never cast a shooting head before, chances are, you have no idea how humbling the process can be. Take the best fly caster in the world– if he's never cast a shooting head, he'll look like Charles Barkley learning how to swing a golf club. (Go look that one up on YouTube.)

I've taught many anglers how to properly cast heads. It's a long process that requires a lot of patience. From the angler and the guide. To make it even more difficult, on the Sac, we really need to cast a minimum of 40 feet for a chance at a striper. Often the angler with the farthest cast catches the most fish. For example, with one angler casting 40 feet and a second at 60 feet, the second may catch twice as many fish.

The good news is, once the shooting head is mastered, casting long distances becomes much easier. But the learning curve can be steep and full of frustration.

Ben noticed the shooting heads as I strung them through the guides of the rods.

"What kind of fly line is *that*?" he asked.

"This is a heavy shooting head with a 30-foot sinking tip. It'll help your fly sink and stay in the zone," I replied.

"Huh, never seen one of those before," Ben said. "I've fished all over the world, but only with floating lines. Gonna be new for me."

As soon as those words came out of Ben's mouth, I knew it would be a long day. Eventually I got all the rods lined up and the boat in the water. Pushing the throttle down on my jet boat, we ripped up the river to a big, open spot for the shooting head casting lesson.

I killed the motor, spot-locked the trolling motor, and gave my normal casting lesson. After going over the particulars for about 10 minutes, Ben chimed in.

"Pretty basic stuff here, Ryan," he said. "I've been fly fishing my whole life. I cast pretty well. I don't understand why you're going into so much detail."

"Well, I know you think you're a good caster. With a floating line. And I'm making this look really easy. But if you haven't cast a shooting head, you have no idea what you're getting into. You're gonna look like Shaquille O'Neal trying to shoot free throws," I said.

Ben laughed. After a few more minutes of explaining the basics, it was time for Ben to take the platform and begin his shooting head journey.

As expected, the first few casts were as bad as Shaq's free throws. After a few more casts, Ben was realizing that all his years of fly fishing hadn't prepared him for the uphill battle of the shooting head. It's a strange conundrum when casting doesn't feel like…casting.

Cast after cast was a struggle. At first, he wasn't even getting the shooting head out of the rod tip; the cast was falling at 25 feet. After a few more minutes and some coaching, his cast improved a bit. Then, about half an hour later, he was finally casting 40 feet—far enough to start his search for his first striper.

It was time to make our way down to the first good striper spot. When teaching anglers how to fish shooting heads, I like to take them to spots that are small and intimate, where casts don't have to be perfect and a 40-footer has a legitimate chance of catching a fish. Ben stood up on the bow and ripped line off his reel for the first cast, which landed about 25 feet from the boat in a sloppy pile of slack.

With a look of frustration, Ben stripped in his line and started another cast. Surprisingly, the second cast was solid and shot out 45 feet. He let the line sink for 8 to 10 seconds, then aggressively started stripping. On his fifth strip, the fly got hammered.

Ben was hooked up on his first striper!

He beamed as he felt the power of the striper bending his 9-weight deep into the butt of the rod. He fought the fish for a few minutes, then landed a nice 7-pound striped bass. It wasn't a big one by any means, but a nice way to start the day. Ben caught four more fish in that small spot; once he stopped getting strikes, we decided it was best to move on.

The second spot of the day was devoid of fish, as were the third and fourth spots.

As Ben and I searched different spots in the river, we talked about winning championships, the struggles of being famous, and the unique life the NBA had provided him.

By this point, it was obvious we had found a few eager fish in the first spot, but in general, the river wasn't fishing well yet. It was only a matter of time before the stripers would wake up.

After the fifth spot didn't yield any willing biters, Ben looked over at me.

"Man, this striper thing is hard," he said. "If we were fishing in Alaska, I would have landed 20 rainbows by now."

I nodded my head. "Just keep focusing on your casting," I told him. "Try to get better. Once the fish wake up, you'll wanna be casting as much line as you possibly can."

Ben continued, and struggled some, with most of his casts landing short of our 40-foot goal. Finally, after two hours with no bites, Ben lucked into a couple more willing stripers.

Over the next several hours, we fished all my smaller spots where casting isn't crucial. After minimal success, I was forced to start fishing the larger, open water in search of another school of fish. The problem with the open water is it takes a longer cast to do well, so I knew our chance of catching more stripers was diminishing.

Ben was giving it everything. With his new casting still under development, the spots left for us were extremely limited. Another hour went by without a bite.

Ben chirped up again.

"You know, if I was in Alaska, my arm would be sore from reeling in so many fish by now," he said.

"Yeah…I know. Just keep casting," I told him. "Try to push yourself to that 50-foot cast."

Ben nodded, but his limitations were real. If he couldn't get that cast to go 10 more feet, we would continue to struggle.

Another hour passed with no more grabs. I started wondering if the fishing was off, or if Ben's new cast was the real issue. Just then, I got a text from one of my guide buddies. "Hammering them upriver!" he reported. Thankful for the intel, I determined the fish were not to blame, but rather the steep learning curve of the shooting head.

Ben was striving to improve. His previous fly fishing experience wasn't transferring to the current situation as much as he hoped. I could feel the energy in the boat shift. Excitement about new skills and first stripers morphed into a lack of confidence and perhaps some pessimism.

"This is why I don't fish in the Lower 48 anymore," Ben said. "The fishing down here sucks. There's nothing like Alaska. Ryan, do you know I've had 100-fish days in Alaska? We hook so many fish up there, you lose count. That's why I'm going there for 3 straight weeks next month."

"Man, I know you're struggling with the casting. But that doesn't mean the fishing sucks. Actually, my buddy upriver is doing really well," I told him. "Since you don't have the casting figured out, we can't cover enough water to present your fly to the fish. The striper fishing here is actually really good. You're just not used to casting the shooting head. Everything you're struggling with is super common for a lot of anglers. Don't beat yourself up."

"Even if this place is as good as you say, it's no Alaska!" Ben replied.

"Yeah, Alaska is magic. I never met an angler who didn't love fishing up there. You can go back year after year, and it rarely disappoints. But if you compare every fishery to Alaska, you'll constantly be disappointed. There's a lot of really cool fisheries in the Lower 48, but you have to adjust your perspective. Keeping Alaska as your benchmark will lead to lots of disappointment."

As he made another cast, Ben muttered, "This is the hardest fishing I've ever done. Fishing in Alaska is easy. This is hard."

That was just about enough Alaska for me, and I love Alaska. Maybe I could help him see he wasn't comparing apples to apples.

"How about an analogy that might put this into perspective for you?" I asked. "Fishing in Alaska is like being with a swimsuit model. After an experience like that, it's gonna be hard to lower the bar back to normal. How can a normal beautiful woman compete? Both are *good*, but they're not the same. You fell in love with Alaska fishing and scorned all these other amazing fisheries we're blessed with in the U.S. You're so focused on catching '100 fish a day,' you're missing all the regular beautiful women right here in front of you."

Ben chuckled and looked over at me with a grin on his face.

"Well, what can I say? I love swimsuit models."

I laughed. "I hear ya," I said.

Ben ended up catching a few more stripers that day, but he wasn't quite satisfied. I guess our good ol' Sacramento River didn't put out enough for him. Ben's Alaska-skewed expectations, or enamor for the Alaskan experience, kinda set him up for disappointment from the start. He did battle through the learning curve of casting shooting heads, and he did achieve his goal of catching his first striper.

To most anglers, that would be a very satisfying victory. But Ben was caught longing for the sexiness of Alaska.

Oh, Alaska…

PRIVILEGED WATERS

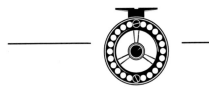

If you have a social media account of any kind, you likely follow one or two fly fishers who post only monster fish to their pages—the guys and gals who land so many badass fish, it makes you wonder what a life like that must feel like. These are the folks who go on countless destination trips a year, posting one sweet video or photo after another from places most of us will only ever dream of: mouse fishing in Alaska, casting large dry flies to rising brown trout in Patagonia, tailing permit in Belize, teasing sailfish on the fly in Costa Rica. The bucket-list spots go on indefinitely.

It must be nice to fish only the top destinations of the world continuously throughout the year. I've had several clients over the years who do annual trips to the Seychelles for big giant trevally, Christmas Island for endless bonefish, Alaska for monster rainbows, and British Columbia for some of the largest steelhead in the world. Then, when these select few anglers get bored at home, they hire me for a handful of days of local trout and steelhead fishing. Having chosen the path of fly fishing guide, I can tell you those destinations are outside of my budget. One day, when I hit the mega-lotto, I'll go on quarterly trips with my family and friends to the wonders of the fly fishing world. One can hope, right? Guess I better start buying lotto tickets.

Over the years, I've had lots of interesting interactions with clients who have fished all over the world, but one day stands out from the rest. I met Mark while guiding for a great lodge on the Snake River in Idaho. Mark was an avid angler in his early 60s. He had spent half of his life chasing exotic fish all over the planet. That morning, in his blue button-up, short-sleeve Orvis shirt, khaki pants and brown leather loafers, he certainly fit the part of a wealthy man who had come to a beautiful high-end lodge for the week.

Shaggy gray hair, a thin salt-and-pepper beard, glasses, and a huge, warm smile… I loved his smile. Mark would have made the perfect cover model for the summer issue of AARP magazine. After introducing ourselves and chatting for a few moments in the fly shop, and buying some flies, we hopped into my truck and headed to the river.

As we rode along the highway to the boat launch, we exchanged pleasantries and talked about all of the incredible fishing trips Mark had recently been on. The week prior, he had visited one of the most coveted private trout rivers in all of Colorado. This particular river is completely private; anglers must pay an expensive access fee and are also required to hire a guide. You're looking at easily $2,000 per day. That's a lot of money to go trout fishing for most anglers, but when the river is loaded with 10-pound trout, some people are willing and able to pay the piper. Mark spent 5 days there and landed 3 rainbows over 10 pounds, the largest weighing 13 pounds. He was happy to show me the pictures of his river monsters.

As I drooled over the impressive photos, I hoped Mark wasn't expecting to catch fish like that on the Snake. No client of mine had ever landed a trout that big in my entire guiding career. Granted, I've seen trout in the 8- to 9-pound range, but I've never had a client land a trout 10 pounds or greater.

We got to the river and Mark strung up his rod while I got the boat prepared for the day. After a few minutes, we were on the water, floating my favorite section of the Snake River, near Idaho Falls. This particular stretch was famous for having lots of hungry brown trout that liked to feed on stoneflies falling from the grassy banks and log jams. Mark had timed the golden stonefly hatch perfectly; I was stoked for him. There were lots of bugs out, and the recent fishing had been incredible. Not private-water-in-Colorado incredible, but seriously awesome, nonetheless.

I tied a tan Chubby Chernobyl Ant onto Mark's leader and we started fishing. Within a few minutes, it was easy to see that Mark was a decent fisherman. He wasn't the best angler I'd ever had in my boat, but he also wasn't the worst. His cast needed a little improvement (whose doesn't?), but most of the time the fly landed close to where it needed to be.

Soon the first brown trout rose up from the grassy undercut bank and smashed Mark's stonefly. He was thrilled watching all the brown trout rise from the shadows, coming to inspect his offering. Some would give him the finger, communicating through fish sign language, "Get outta here!" Others would come up, nudge the fly, checking if it was real or not. "I'm no fool!" Every fourth fish would crush his fly so hard, you'd wonder if that trout had eaten all week.

After a while, we got downriver to a log jam that consistently had a group of fish rising behind it all week. These fish had been feeding more than a fat man at Hometown Buffet. The sheer number of stoneflies falling off this log had every trout in the 50-foot pocket looking up and gorging themselves. I rowed past the large, protruding log jam and then reached out to hold onto the bottom of the log.

As I held the boat in place, I said to Mark, "Look up behind the log jam. Do you see where that current line is coming off the top branch? Right on that current seam, you should see a buncha fish rising. There's one... another one... oh, right there... you see 'em?"

"Yep, I see 'em," he replied.

"Okay, go ahead and make a good cast just off that top branch," I told him. "As soon as your fly settles on the water, you're gonna have to pull in your slack, as your fly floats toward you. That should be an automatic hook up right there. If we get lucky, and the fish you hook doesn't rip off toward the middle of the river, we could catch quite a few outta here."

Mark began his cast forward. His fly landed about three feet to the left of the branch. The fish didn't respond.

"This time try to get your fly right off the tip of the branch," I said. "That last cast went too far left."

Mark's second cast was much better. It landed softly in the current seam behind the branch. However, as his fly began to float toward him, he forgot to strip in his extra slack. A nice brown came up and chomped his fly. Mark quickly threw his hand up to set the hook—but he set the hook on slack.

Mark's eyes met mine in disappointment.

"Don't worry about that one," I told him. "There are easily a dozen fish in there. Get the next one. Just remember to strip in your slack as your fly is floating toward you."

Mark made his third cast in the same spot. This time he was focused on his slack; he started stripping as soon as the fly hit the water. However, rather than allowing the fly to settle before slowly pulling the slack in, he was now skittering his dry fly across the surface of the water, stripping so quickly that his Chernobyl Ant looked more like a bass popper.

"That was a good cast, Mark," I said. "Next time, don't be so aggressive with your stripping. Let the fly float naturally, like a real insect."

With his fourth cast, Mark's leader landed on the end of a branch. His fly instantly acted like a Ferris Wheel, going round and round and round, tying itself in multiple tight loops around the branch.

"Ah, man! Sorry, Mark! Go ahead and break your fly off. I don't want to row up there and scare all these fish away," I said. "There's alotta hungry and willing trout in there if we can get this done. Go ahead an' hold the branch. I'll tie a new fly on for you."

Mark reached out and grabbed the branch. I took his frayed leader and attached some new tippet to the end, choosing another fly to tie on. Since the Chubby Chernobyl Ant had been so productive all morning, and for the previous week, I tied on another.

Mark let go of the branch, gathered himself and started another cast. To both of our surprise, his next cast landed in the exact same spot as the one before. His fly was like an insect attracted to a bright light. The magnetic pull of the log sent Mark's second fly to be with its long-lost friend, hanging on for dear life over the water.

"All right, Mark. No problem. Go ahead and break that fly off again. I'll get you a new one," I said.

After a few minutes of re-rigging, Mark was back in the game. His next cast missed the branch and landed a couple feet too far to the right.

The following cast, though, was PERFECT, landing exactly where it needed to be.

As the fly began to settle, Mark sloooowly stripped in his line.

The fly danced on the current line. Slowly, from the depths, a long snout emerged from the water to lazily eat it. Mark set the hook as soon as he saw the snout...and pulled the fly away before the fish had a chance to eat it. Gut punch. Mark's head fell to his chest, knowing he had missed a good one.

We sat in that spot for more than 45 minutes, watching multiple fish rise every minute. The fish were ready and willing, but every time Mark put a cast behind the log jam, he did something wrong. He was trying to put all of the pieces of the puzzle together, but he was struggling. He would do one thing really well and then miss something else.

Mark turned around to me with that big smile.

"Ryan, fishing in public water is hard," he said. "I'm used to fishing private waters where the fish don't get fished over every day. I think this spot is above my paygrade."

I smiled back at him. "Yep, sadly, these fish see a lot of flies," I said. "You were really close to catching a couple! Not as easy as fishing private waters, for sure. And it's definitely not as good as Patagonia." I laughed.

As soon as I said the word "Patagonia," Mark's whole face lit up. "Ryan, have you ever been to Patagonia?"

I shook my head no.

"Oh my gosh. You have got to go there," he said. "It might be some of the best trout fishing on the entire planet. You have to see these pictures – some of the monster brown trout I caught there last winter."

Mark reached into his bag and pulled out his phone. He scrolled through a year's worth of photos to show me the 9-pound brown trout he landed on a hopper. Handing me his phone, he told me to scroll to the left.

There, as we floated down one of the West's premier dry fly fisheries, Mark was getting lost in his pictures from all the other fisheries.

"Pretty incredible fish," I told him. "I hope I can get down there one day. Patagonia is definitely on my bucket list."

"If you think those fish are great," said Mark, "you should see the picture of the brown trout I caught in New Zealand."

As Mark scrolled through his phone once more, I reminisced about all my years of guiding. I can't help but want to be the guy who only goes to badass fishing spots, but then I remember that there are a lot of people who would like to be in my shoes, spending a lifetime pursuing their passion in the great outdoors. I feel honored and privileged to know that I have experienced a lot – that a lot of people only dream about.

When you spend two decades on the river chasing fish,

there are plenty of interesting and unique situations to experience. They won't all be 10-pound-trout-on-a-dry-fly experiences, but being charged by a moose, losing oars in the middle of the river, having anglers fall out of the boat, and removing flies from various body parts of various people are all memorable moments I truly appreciate. Removing a large stonefly hook from one particular client's ass was definitely unforgettable.

I'm aware that the grass is not always greener on the other side. That said, casting dry flies at monster browns in Patagonia sounds pretty damn awesome to me. I guess it's time to go buy that lotto ticket.

CHASING UNICORNS

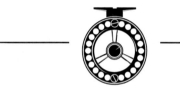

Do you believe in unicorns? I know my young daughters used to. I'm still on the fence with the idea, but there is a small part of me that wants to believe. I believe in Bigfoot and the Loch Ness Monster, so why not unicorns as well?

When you look up the word "unicorn" in the dictionary, there are two definitions. The first is the one we all instantly think of: *A mythical animal typically represented as a horse with a single straight horn projecting from its forehead.* Any fish enthusiast might think, by that definition, that a narwhal would then be the unicorn of the fish world. But the second definition of "unicorn" actually seems to be more suggestive of steelhead over narwhals: *Something that is highly desirable but difficult to find or obtain.* That is the best synopsis of steelhead fishing I've ever seen.

We see photos in magazines and on social media of mystically huge anadromous rainbow trout caught from breathtaking rivers in some of the world's most pristine environments. Pictures of big, chrome-bright, 20-pound steelhead that make us wish for the umpteenth time that we had more money to travel more, to more faraway lands, more time to chase after more fish we're not entirely sure exist, and also maybe spouses who could understand our madness. Just a little?

As we stare into the eyes of that person smiling ear to ear, holding that fish that lives only in our dreams, we drift away to enchanted steelhead lands surrounded by rugged, snow-capped mountains towering over rivers that flow through mighty redwoods and foggy rain forests. Clean, fresh, cold water glows a perfect emerald green, the weather is always dry and cloudy, the sun never comes out to scare the fish, and the wind never blows to affect our casts. Fog slowly rolling in and out to keep a perfectly moist yet brisk feeling in our lungs. Perfect holding water in every run; big, bright unicorns rolling in every tailout. Now I'm starting to wonder if this is what Heaven will be like.

The cell phone dings, awakening me from my mental wonderland, and I'm sadly confronted by the reality that a place like this doesn't exist. Not earthside anyway. Even the most desirable steelhead destinations in the world get adverse conditions. Yes, there are rivers where thousands of wild steelhead return every year. Yes, there are rivers that flow through the most beautiful and dramatic and almost unimaginable scenery. Yes, there are days when all the planets and stars in the universe align to produce the perfect conditions. But when you go looking for unicorns, brace yourself: be prepared to be disappointed.

Steelhead chasing is like that. A lot of our time is just hoping to interact with one. In every run we fish, we keep hoping and believing there's a unicorn waiting to reveal itself in all its splendor. A fresh steelhead that ever so briefly lets its guard down, eats our fly, and reveals mythical powers so strong it must be from another world entirely.

Steelhead swim with speed akin to bonefish, though they are much stronger than those flats dwellers. The bonefish is bit of a waif-like Olympic sprinter; it doesn't have long-distance endurance. Bonefish will rip that line right off your reel with blazing speed, but they tire easily. Steelhead have that kind of speed but the tenacity of a King Salmon.

King Salmon regularly test the will of anglers all over the world. When hooked, they never give up. They're like the strongest guy at the gym. You go in for your routine hour-long workout, but then there's that guy- the strongest guy, he's there for four hours at a time, every day, twice a day, getting stronger and bigger than you. The King Salmon keeps tugging and pulling until every ounce of energy has left its body, and its energy bank is impressive. Steelhead and salmon are very similar in that they don't give up quickly or easily.

But unlike the salmon, the steelhead's instincts are more erratic, similar to the dorado. Dorado, also known as mahi mahi in Hawaii and dolphin on the East Coast, are one of the world's most unpredictable game fish. When hooked, they go on long runs with lots of jumping. One moment they're ripping line to the right, seconds later they're throwing their bodies out of the water in an effort to escape, then, in an instant, they're jetting straight toward you. You think you have them under control, then another burst of energy comes and they do something completely different. Kinda like a toddler at bedtime. They're famous for their big aerial displays and speed.

The steelhead is the perfect freshwater unicorn in its thrilling combination of the gifts of all these world-renowned gamefish. It has the speed of a bonefish, the strength and stamina of a King Salmon, and the erratic, wild fight of a dorado. It is a fish so perfect, anglers will do almost anything to engage one.

A few years ago, a couple clients of mine were seeking their first unicorn in the Redwood National Forest on California's north coast. Matt and Roy had been fishing with me for a long time, and we had caught lots of trout, stripers, and bass together. They're good fishermen. Also, like all of us, they still had some things to learn. Each had been fly fishing for about five years and were gradually becoming more proficient at the sport. It was time to go land their first steelheads on the Eel River.

The first day of the trip went well enough. Matt hooked three steelhead, though he didn't land any. The first was a beautiful 13ish-pound, chrome-bright buck, fought perfectly all the way to the boat... where the hook pulled out two feet from the net. The fish was so close, but the never-give-up attitude of the steelhead won.

Two hours later, Matt hooked his second unicorn. We were nymphing through a deep, emerald-green run. As soon as the fly fell off the shelf, the indicator shot under the water. Matt, with lightning-quick reflexes, set the hook and came tight to something big and strong. The fish jetted upriver, instantly jumping all the fly line off the deck of the boat. The reel engaged and the fish continued to pull an additional 30 feet of line upriver. In an instant, the steelhead decided to change directions and made a bee line for Matt.

I started yelling at him. "Reel faster!!! Keep up with him!" Matt was cranking hard, but nothing changed. I looked over my shoulder to investigate and noticed he was reeling backwards! Rather than picking up the slack, he was making a bird's nest in his reel, and the fish came off.

"What happened there?" asked Roy, annoyed that Matt had hooked the first two steelhead of the day, with none yet for himself. "How did you lose that one?"

"The only explanation for Matt losing that fish is LOFT," I said.

"Loft?" asked Roy. "I've never heard that term before."

"LOFT is an acronym used widely amongst fly fishing guides," I said. "Lack of Fucking Talent."

Roy instantly laughed and nodded his head in agreement. After my dumb guide joke, I rowed down to the next run in hopes of actually landing one of these unicorns.

Hours later, Matt had his third hookup of the day. He set the hook hard. His rod pulsed from the big headshakes of the fish. So captivating was the power of that coveted creature, Matt forgot to strip his line to maintain tension. Sadly, the magnificent and intelligent steelhead dislodged the hook and escaped.

Matt had three chances to catch his first unicorn, and the fish managed to escape every time. We would occasionally get glimpses of these beautiful unicorns, but each time they would slowly sulk down into the depths of the run to hide from us. Steelhead have the unique ability of frequently evading an angler's line. Even the best anglers in the world only land half of the steelhead they hook. Every step must be executed to absolute perfection with flawless finesse.

We would spend the rest of the day searching and fishing

every hole. Our efforts proved futile; we were never able to hook a fourth fish. By steelhead standards, it was a great day of fishing. But my anglers were disappointed they didn't land any of them. Matt had three solid chances and Roy never had a bite.

The next day, we visited a different section of the river. We fished hard in absolutely perfect conditions and never had one chance. It was the first time in my 18 years of guiding that my clients never hooked a fish. I was devastated. But I knew it was only a matter of time before my good luck streak would come to an end. This was that day.

On the drive home, I insisted Roy needed to give it another shot. I really wanted him to. "Come back with me next time the fishing conditions are right."

Just our luck, the following month, the coastal rivers were coming into good shape for another unicorn hunt, so I called him. "Roy! The next few days are prime steelhead conditions. The weather and water conditions are gonna be great. Can you come up and try again?"

Roy made some adjustments to his calendar, and three days later we were hunting unicorns on the Eel River again.

The level of anticipation was high as we started our search. Roy fished hard. He made challenging casts into spots most anglers wouldn't be able to reach. He paid close attention to his indicator, looking for the smallest twitch. Hour after hour, he waited in anticipation. Before we knew it, the sun was starting to set.

And just like that, I had TWO client days of nothing. Nada. Zilch. With our heads hung a little low, we went to bed with a strong plan for the following day.

The next day, to our dismay, we experienced the same results.

The conditions on the river were great, but we couldn't find any fish. Roy had now logged *four* long, hard days of steelhead fishing without finding his unicorn.

I started to wonder if Roy had a steelhead curse. Maybe the fish gods were punishing him for all the years of torturing other fish species. I quickly shook that idea out of my head, as I don't believe in curses. I may believe in mythical creatures, but curses are bullshit excuses for people who can't catch fish.

I was determined to get Roy his unicorn. Whether from bitterness or stubborn will, I wasn't gonna let this guy *not* catch a steelhead. This journey had become personal for me; I was supposed to be The One to Help Roy Catch His First Steelhead.

I checked my calendar. There was one day open the following week. I offered it to him, begged him to come back for one last try. "If you don't hook a fish, the day's on me." I couldn't let him give up, because I couldn't give up; landing your first steelhead is a fantastic experience, not something a fellow angler lets his comrade let go of.

Roy agreed to come up for one more day. "But this is it. If I don't catch one on my fifth try, I'm laying it down. No more chasing unicorns."

Six days later we found ourselves back on the river with all the pressure in the world on my shoulders. The river was becoming low and clear—tough conditions for catching steelhead. The fish become more alert, hiding near rocks for protection.

We launched early in the morning and started fishing as the sun rose through the towering redwood trees. Several hours passed with no luck; it was like a misty ghost town. Then, all of a sudden, the steelhead stars aligned, and Roy's indicator shot under the water.

A quick, firm hookset sent a big, bright steelhead rocketing out of the water.

Roy perfectly counteracted every erratic move the fish made. It was like he had been rehearsing this fight in his dreams. The steelhead began to tire.

I stood perched, and readied my net. The fish was exhausted. Then, incredibly, the steelhead made one last-ditch effort to thrash its head around, desperate to dislodge that hook.

Roy and I watched in utter shock as the fish slowly, smoothly swam back into the darkness, never to be seen again.

This called for an anchor. I pulled to the bank and checked Roy's leader. But really it was so we could gather ourselves. That was our chance, we both knew it. But, just like getting knocked down in a boxing match, you have to get back on your feet to throw another punch. So we didn't stay long. I pushed the boat off the bank and rowed downriver to the next hole.

Roy was quiet for the next 10 minutes. He just stared off in the distance, slowly replaying the story in his mind. When we got to the next run, he stood up and started fishing again. Hoping for another one.

That run didn't have any willing fish, nor did the one after that. We fished for hours with no luck. As time ticked by, we both felt the doubt creeping in. Roy was no longer fishing well. His hook sets were weak; he wasn't always paying attention. There were multiple times I reminded him to keep trying, to keep believing. My role had evolved from fishing guide to fishing coach as I encouraged Roy to keep his head in the game.

To his credit, Roy kept trying. He was trying to be hopeful, but keeping hope alive in the face of ever decreasing odds is a fight in itself. We were now within sight of the takeout spot.

There were only two runs left before Roy would give up on unicorn hunting for good.

As we fished through the second-to-the-last run, I was allowing his flies to float down into the super-slow water, desperate to sneak up on a steelhead resting. As the indicator slowly floated, it twitched slightly.

Then it violently shot under the water.

Roy set the hook hard and the steelhead ran directly at him. It had been an emotional day. Roy was tired. He forgot to strip his line. Without the proper amount of tension, the fish was able to escape.

Roy slumped down into his chair. He looked as if he had just struck out to lose the game. My coach instincts took over.

"Get up and try again. We have one more spot. You're not out of water yet. C'mon, let's go get it."

I knew our chances were slim as hell as we floated to the last spot. No client of mine had ever caught a steelhead in this run.

Roy stood up and put a good cast in the far seam on the bank. His indicator floated about 20 feet as it danced its way around the eddy in the foam of the bank. To my total surprise, his indicator went under the water. Roy set the hook hard and fast...

ROY HAD HOOKED THE MIRACLE FISH.

Hooking a fish at the takeout? Do you know how rare it is to hook a fish at the takeout?!

The fish was cartwheeling under the water, determined to free itself. In the excitement and shock of it all, once again, Roy forgot to strip his line to stay tight. For a few brief seconds, he had his third chance of the day, until once again his unicorn escaped.

He released his frustration in a huge roar. He'd had the

chances, but didn't capitalize on any of them. The closer had thrown a fastball right down the middle of the plate. He whiffed.

It caught up to me as well. I was so frustrated that he had lost another fish. I had one mission that day, and I had gotten so close. I was working my ass off, but the steelhead curse was working against us. I looked up at Roy in agony.

"Dude! What the hell! You have to strip. Stripping is such a basic part of fly fishing. How do you forget to strip on two fish in a row?"

With just enough time for one last-ditch effort, I slowly rowed back to the top of the run. Roy cast into the run for a second time. This time, we went all the way through the run. And right at the last possible second, Roy's indicator went down.

This time, Roy stripped like a mad man.

A huge, 15-pound steelhead rocketed out of the water, swimming downriver like the Millenium Falcon. Jump after jump, it tried to get away, but the fish gods finally decided they had put Roy through enough agony and turmoil. He had earned this one.

The steelhead tried every move to get free, but Roy was ready this time, and desperate enough. He landed the beautiful unicorn.

As we stood there looking at the incredible fish in the water, our eyes met. Our smiles shone as bright as the fish, and we embraced with joy and relief in a celebratory bear hug.

Of course there were victory photos. Not that we needed them to help us remember. How could we forget this journey, this fight to the end? They were more like the only trophy we could find.

Roy released his unicorn back into the river. After the fish swam away, we both stood there in awe and pure ecstasy as we took in the magnitude of the moment.

Roy and I now go hunting for unicorns every year on California's coastal rivers. He broke the steelhead curse, so now he usually lands a couple of fish every time we go. Roy has actually become a passionate steelhead angler, understanding the addiction, why some people will sacrifice their jobs, relationships, physical bodies, and mental state in hopes of having a brief interaction with these fish. Roy, like many addicted people, will do just about anything to get his fix.

Hunting for unicorns isn't for the faint of heart. You may spend days or weeks trying to get a glimpse of one. When your time comes, though, and the fish gods bless you with that mysterious ocean-running creature, I hope you'll enjoy every moment of it. And remember to strip.

OBSESSION

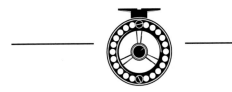

In the world of fly fishing, there are four types of anglers. These anglers share a passion so profound, they will travel the world, risking their jobs, their marriages, and their life's savings in an attempt for one more hook-up.

The four types of anglers are permit fishermen, tarpon fishermen, Atlantic salmon fishermen, and steelheaders. Each of these anglers has a certain edge about them, with gritty similarities. Even though the fish they chase live in different environments and locations, these anglers are one and the same, and there is only one word to describe them: Obsessed.

I have spent half of my life chasing steelhead, and I can tell you that I am obsessed. A steelheader, like an alcoholic or drug addict, just wants another hit. While these addicts may look different, they have similar, intertwined roots to their chosen vice. An alcoholic needs a drink to calm the nerves, a drug addict needs another hit to feel right, and a steelheader needs one more tug to fill an insatiable desire.

Outsiders may not understand how an angler can become so obsessed with a fish, but when the obsession is characterized as an addiction, it starts to make sense. Even though fishing is socially acceptable, a steelhead addiction has the ability to bring you to the highest of highs and the lowest of lows. There will be times when you feel like you are standing on a mountaintop, and others when you will question the state of your mental health. The steelhead is not the fish you want to chase if you want to be considered a healthy human being.

The steelhead is an anadromous rainbow trout born in freshwater, migrates to saltwater, and then returns to freshwater to spawn. Due to the steelhead's migratory journey, it becomes a strong and resilient fish. Steelhead are famous worldwide for line-peeling runs and spectacular, acrobatic fights. They are often described as elusive, challenging, and the ultimate freshwater game fish. Just a total badass, really.

Hooking a steelhead produces an energy that is hard to define—it's like a bolt of lightning pulsing through the rod. The energy is so strong and sudden that it almost jerks the rod out of your hand on contact. As soon as you come tight to this mysterious, ocean-going creature, pure chaos ensues. No control, no predicting, you're just trying to stay on the ride. STAY ON THE RIDE.

Two earthly creatures come into total and direct conflict with each other.

For the steelhead, its goal of swimming upriver to spawn and create a new generation of fish is now suddenly in jeopardy.

For the angler, a huge hit of dopamine floods his brain as he watches and feels the steelhead surge across the river, stealing liberty.

Indeed, dopamine is the real root of the steelhead addiction. A neurotransmitter (chemical) made in the brain, dopamine basically acts as a chemical messenger between brain cells, released when our brains expect a reward. For the angler, dopamine is released when he comes tight to a fish. He knows he has presented his fly well enough to fool the fish. As the fish runs and jumps, the angler's brain releases additional dopamine to make him feel good.

When we come to associate a certain activity with pleasure, in this case fly fishing, mere anticipation may be enough to raise our dopamine levels. That's why we get a feeling of excitement when we read fishing magazines and catalogs or scroll through fishing photos on social media. For many people, increased dopamine levels come from food, intimacy, shopping, exercise, or just about anything a person enjoys. For the fisherman, it comes on the water when catching a fish.

A flood of dopamine can produce temporary feelings of euphoria. It can come from hitting the game-winning shot or getting the phone number of the most beautiful girl you've ever seen. This abundance of dopamine makes us feel like we're on top of the world. For the steelhead angler, this would be when the biggest fish of your life is scooped up in the net. Your friends hoot and holler wildly as you pump your fists in the air. You know you have mastered the unicorn, overcome insanely low odds, and finally won the battle.

The thing about a steelhead addiction is that once we land a fish of a lifetime, all we want is another one. The feeling of euphoria we get from bringing a monster fish to hand may last an hour, a day, or even a month, but in time the urge of wanting a bigger, faster, or crazier fish starts to creep up. It's never enough. Just as nicotine, alcohol, cocaine, and other drugs with addictive qualities activate the dopamine cycle, steelhead fishing is no different.

I would argue a steelhead creates a far more intense dopamine rush than we might get from, say, fishing for brook trout on a small creek. It's such a powerful rush that we're left wanting more — and soon. I don't know many bluegill fishermen that just can't wait for their next trip. A bluegill doesn't get your heart pounding out of your chest.

As the steelheading habit forms, the brain responds by toning down the dopamine levels that are released into the body. We need more steelhead experiences to get to that same pleasure level. The first 10-pound steelhead landed provides a euphoric experience, but over time the level of euphoria starts to diminish, leaving us wanting something bigger and better.

This is where overactivation starts to take shape. Falling deeper and deeper into the black hole of steelhead addiction, we lose interest in our local steelhead scene. The river down the road no longer gives the same euphoric dopamine hits, and the brain starts to crave trips to the Olympic Peninsula, British Columbia, Kamchatka.

10-pounders become less provocative. Now we need a 20-pounder to get the fix. What we really want is to catch the fish on the cover of a magazine. We begin to act more compulsively. The steelhead brain starts to compromise the ability to make sound decisions. The thought of spending five figures on a fishing trip, even though the kids need braces, begins to sound reasonable. The idea of skipping out on your wedding anniversary because the river flows are about to be perfect starts to enter your mind. *My wife will be fine. Our anniversary can wait a week.*

The fish-crazed mind is becoming less and less able to resist these massive steelhead dopamine hits. The desire to chase steelhead becomes more of a need than a want. Trying to stop the chase causes physical and emotional symptoms of withdrawal. Smokers can try a nicotine patch to help with cravings and withdrawal symptoms, but there is nothing quite like having that cigarette between their fingers. Similarly, trout fishing may ease the ache, but the pleasure could never compare to a steelhead!

Some people will never understand. (Trust me, your spouse really won't, even if you compare it to…chocolate. Or shoes.). They will look at steelhead anglers and question their sanity. They won't understand why someone wants, no needs, to stand in the freezing rain for 8 hours just for a brief encounter with a fish. They won't understand waking at 2am and driving 5 hours in hopes of finding an emerald-green river. They won't understand the hundreds of casts to possibly hook a single fish. If you haven't done it, you will never get it.

Steelheaders, like those that chase Atlantic salmon, permit, and tarpon, are a rare breed of hard-core anglers. They will go to the ends of the earth to have brief but eternally memorable encounters with these special fish. They will endure adverse and painful conditions for a euphoric dopamine hit to feed their addiction. This is, after all, why steelheaders all over the world say, "The tug is the drug."

WALK-OFF

Few things rival the excitement of a walk-off win. Whether it's a go-ahead three-pointer at the buzzer, a last-second field goal, or a homerun in the bottom of the ninth, these moments could be considered among the most thrilling in sports. As a fan, I love "game 7's," underdog teams, and big comebacks. Watching history play out before your eyes- that's exciting. The drama of the "practically impossible" happening, a team – *your* team – overcoming adversity at the last possible second...this is the good stuff.

When it comes to fishing, don't we always hope for a walk-off fish? The best way to exit the water is right after one last tug. At the end of an outing, how many of us tell ourselves, "Just one more cast"? And when that doesn't produce a fish, maybe we convince ourselves there's time for just one or two more. After all, what's the harm in being five minutes late to a meeting? …eating a slightly-less-warm meal? …missing the first few minutes of a church service?

To be honest, or let's say *accurate*, rarely does the last cast result in a fish. But we want so badly to finish the trip with a victory! Certainly there's a chance to hit a walk-off! And every additional cast increases the probability. Simple math.

The batter who strikes out to end the baseball game can't ask for three more pitches. But we often try to negotiate with the fish: *Just one little taste…just this once…I promise to let you go…* And occasionally, the fish throws you a fastball right down the middle of the plate, and you hammer that last cast. You come tight to a beautiful, hard-fighting fish, landed as your glorious finish. Which means the drive home consists of basking in your victory with a smile that just won't quit.

In 20 years of guiding, I have experienced many last-cast fish. Two in particular left me in awe.

The first was a day of trout fishing on the Lower Sacramento River in Northern California. My friend and I were guiding three generations of a family—grandfather Ray Miller, father Mike, and sons Justin and John. It was one of those perfect days on the river, with clear blue skies and no clouds in sight. The air was calm, the bugs were hatching, and the swallows were diving for their next meal.

I had Ray and Justin in my boat; my buddy guided Mike and John. As with most family group trips, we had decided to fish close together. After a few hours, we had already caught a bunch of trout. There was a feeling of merriment in the air as everyone enjoyed one another's success.

Around 11 that morning, Grandpa Ray set the hook hard.

He was instantly connected to something much larger than all the fish we had caught so far. On the initial hookset, the fish rocketed across the river toward the far bank; I started rowing as fast as I could in an effort to keep the fish.

Ray expertly managed his line and kept tension on the fish. For a while, we never saw what Ray had on his line.

Ray kept his rod tip high as he pulled back on the mysterious beast below. After what seemed like an eternity (in reality, probably 7 or 8 minutes), we got our first glimpse of the big rainbow. I instantly estimated it to be 26 to 28 inches.

As the fight continued, my guide buddy rowed over; everyone watched in anticipation. Little by little, Ray would subdue the beast. The fish slowly peeled off the bottom of the river as Ray pulled steadily and directed the rainbow into the net.

"Hell yeah, Gramps!" Justin yelled.

"Holy shit, that is the biggest trout I've ever seen in my entire life!" John added.

At first, Mike just nodded in amazement. "Well done, Dad."

There it was, a 27-inch rainbow resting at the bottom of the net. We all sat there stunned, gazing. Knowing – hoping – this could become a lifetime story for these four men, we rowed to the bank for photos of the three generations of Millers with huge smiles on their faces to match the even huge-er fish. Satisfied, we released the giant back into the water and watched it gently swim away to live another day.

Everyone loaded back into the boats. Ray sat in my front seat. He reeled up his line and hooked up all his flies. Then he reached into his backpack, fumbling around in one of the pockets.

He pulled out a Cuban cigar.

He cut the cigar and lit it, puff-puff-puffing to get it going. Once it was nice and hot, Ray put his feet up on the side of the boat and took a big, long draw from the Cuban. Silently he leaned back, face to the sky, as if thanking God.

With a face lit like the Fourth of July, he turned to his family. "Boys...that's how it's done!"

There was Grandpa and his family, all basking together in his glory. Ray seemed to know that fish was a Lifetime Fish. He never once touched a fly rod the rest of that day. He sat back, smoked his cigar, and had a blast watching his son and grandsons catch rainbow after rainbow. Ray hit the grand slam, won the game, and walked off the biggest winner in the Miller family that day.

The only time I've had an experience close to Ray's was my last day on the Eel River in the Redwood National Forest. I was moving out of state and knew it would be awhile before I would get to guide this river again, if ever. I was in perfect company for Big Day vibes; I was guiding my very good friend and longtime client, Floyd. We were on the hunt for coastal steelhead down low on the main Eel River about 10 miles from the ocean.

It was a cool, cloudy morning; the marine fog was slowly drifting in from the Pacific. The rays of the rising sun penetrated the fog with brilliant colors of orange and pink. We launched the boat that morning with our expectations high. Holding on to the idea that it was my last day guiding that river for the foreseeable future, we both wanted it to end well.

Not much was happening as we fished along that morning. We drifted hole after hole with no luck. High expectations of a Big Day were slapped in the face by the reality check of typical coastal steelhead fishing – that is, difficult. We went all morning with no fish to speak of.

Then, at 1pm, Floyd's indicator shot violently under the water. He set the hook hard. A massive steelhead instantly erupted out of the water like a missile being shot off an aircraft carrier. As the fish put on an aerial show, we both knew Floyd had hooked a good one.

"THAT IS A BIG FISH, MAN!" I yelled in excitement. "Don't screw this one up!"

Floyd, completely in the moment, did everything right.

When the steelhead jumped, he immediately bowed his rod. When it ripped off line faster than a kid chasing an ice cream truck, he let the reel spin out. Every move the steelhead made, Floyd counteracted perfectly. He applied the just-right amount of pressure to his eight-weight rod.

Then, in time, he brought the chrome, ocean-bright steelhead close to the boat.

I slowly lowered the net to the water and proceeded to scoop up the largest steelhead my buddy Floyd had ever landed.

We erupted in excitement, cheering and hugging in celebration. There in the net below us was a 15-pound steelhead, a fish many people only dream about.

We dropped the anchor and got out of the boat to take a handful of photos. Then Floyd gave the fish a chance to recover and slowly released it back to the cold, pristine waters of the redwoods.

We sat there in silence as we watched the fish disappear into the emerald-green steelhead waters. As we relived the moment in our heads, Floyd broke the silence.

"Ryan, that was incredible…"

He paused, then continued.

"That was a really special fish. I've been waiting a long time for that one. We're gonna walk that fish off," he said determinedly.

I looked at him. "What do you mean, we're gonna walk that fish off?" I asked. "We could probably catch another one this afternoon."

"Well, let's be honest," Floyd replied. "Yeah, I know we could probably hook another fish. The reality, though, is I'm probably gonna screw it up. I'll forget to strip, get a knot in my running line, not set the hook hard enough…or some other damn thing I won't do right."

I chuckled at his candor and nodded my head in agreement. "Yeah, you're probably right. These fish do have a way of coming off a lot."

Floyd, with a big smile, said, "Rather than screwing up the next grab, we're gonna head home. That's the biggest steelhead I have *ever* landed. It won't get any better than that. Plus, you're gonna end 20 years of the Eel on that moment! We get to walk off on the highest of highs!"

I sat there pensively, still in disbelief from the catch, but I agreed with him.

"All right, Floyd. Let's do a walk off."

I reached up to Floyd's rod and cut off his flies. He reeled his line in, set the rod down, put his feet up, leaned back, and laced his hands behind his head.

I slowly pushed forward on the oar blades. All we could hear was the slapping of water. We still had three miles to go.

We sat there quietly together, alone in our thoughts, reflecting on what had just happened. Floyd was replaying an incredible interaction with a beautiful steelhead. I was reminiscing on 20 incredible years of fishing that beautiful river. I became emotional as memories of friends and clients flooded my mind.

Each riffle, run, and hole reminded me of all the coastal steelhead landed and lost. Each landmark called a different memory to appear out of the fog as though watching it in real time. The Eel River has been a huge part of my fishing story, a place I hold dear to my heart. All those years of figuring out the intricacies and mysteries of the river ended with a true Lifetime Fish.

As for the walk-offs...they do happen, once in a while. Those last casts don't always produce a fish, but when they do, they're often instantly memorable. And, if you happen to catch a Lifetime Fish, maybe keep in mind that, like Grandpa Ray and Floyd, you can walk it off anytime you'd like.

EXPERTS

What does it mean to be an expert? How about a fly fishing expert?

To me, it means proficiency in many forms of fly fishing for many species of fish. Mastering many techniques in a variety of situations. It means being "good at a lot, knowing a lot."

I consider myself an expert at trout and steelhead fishing. I've spent thousands of days fishing for and catching those species.

However, there are still some techniques and methods I'm not as well versed in. The true beauty of fly fishing is that we'll never "get it" all. New tackle and techniques keep coming, so we'll keep having the opportunity to master new ways of catching fish. And while I might be an expert on the trout and steelhead rivers I fish most, that doesn't mean I'm all-knowing.

An expert doesn't know *everything*. An expert does know a

lot, with a deep understanding of how the "a lot" fits together. Let's be honest: The term "expert" gets tossed around frequently, but the meaning of the term often lies in the perspective of the person using it.

If I'm talking to a beginner angler about fly fishing, then I'm the expert in the situation. If I'm talking to Michael Jordan about basketball, I am no longer the expert, even though I spent my whole childhood playing the sport.

Now two "experts" talking together on one topic can make for an interesting dynamic. Can you imagine the basketball conversations between Michael Jordan and Larry Bird? Or how about the music conversations between Eric Clapton and James Taylor? These conversations can go one of two ways. They can be full of respect and reverence for the other person and their perspective, or they can be filled with pride and arrogance.

I once guided an "expert" fly fisherman while working at a prestigious lodge on the Snake River in Idaho. The manager of the lodge, Sebastian, was a great man – warm, extroverted, intelligent, fun-loving and friendly, savvy in fishing, business, and food – we all enjoyed working for him. Sebastian fit the role of fishing lodge manager perfectly; he had tons of experience in hospitality and guiding.

One June morning, I had just pulled up at the lodge for the day, stepped into the fly shop to get ready for my day of guiding, when Sebastian walked up to me.

"Ryan! Morning! How are ya?"

"Good!" I said smiling. "You?"

"Good, good! Hey, I wanna have a conversation about your clients for the day," he said.

"Okay, what do I need to know?" I responded.

"Today, you are going to be fishing with an expert-level angler," Sebastian said. "His name is Randy. He's owned a fly shop in Colorado for over 30 years. Randy is a great fisherman; he knows a ton. You're gonna be stoked to fish with him."

"Cool," I replied, wondering where this was going.

"So," Sebastian went on, "Randy has made one small request for his guide trip today."

"Ah," I said. "What's that?"

"Randy has requested that his guide not give him any advice," Sebastian explained. "He doesn't want any help. He enjoys doing his own thing, fishing his own hand-tied flies, figuring things out on his own."

"Okay, lemme make sure I got this right. Randy is hiring a guide who knows the Snake really well, but doesn't want any help with it?"

"Yes, that is correct. Just put Randy in the back of your boat and ignore him all day," Sebastian replied. "His friend, Brian, wants help with rigging flies, where to fish, how to fish better. Just do your normal guide program with Brian. And forget about Randy."

"That doesn't make any sense," I said. "I get that he may consider himself an expert fly fisherman, but that doesn't make him an expert on every river. This seems like a trap. But I'll do my best to just guide Brian and let Randy do whatever he wants to do."

"You got it!" Sebastian affirmed, ever the diplomat. I scratched my noggin; this was gonna be a weird day.

A few minutes later, Randy and Brian made their way over. They were both really warm and friendly as we exchanged pleasantries before we hopped into my truck to head down the road.

As we drove to the river, we talked about fly fishing trips that Randy and Brian had done all over the world. These guys had been to lots of international fishing spots but had never fished the Snake. They were excited to cross another acclaimed river off their fly fishing bucket lists.

Unfortunately, Randy and Brian had come in June, before the water temperature had warmed up enough to get the bug hatches going. With the weather and river conditions, we would be forced to fish with indicators and nymphs.

At the boat launch, we all got out of the truck to get ready for the day. I got the boat ready, then switched my attention to rigging up rods. I worked on Brian's rods and simultaneously peeked over at Randy from time to time as he set up his own.

Randy's plan was to fish three flies. He picked out a massive size-2 weighted stonefly, a medium size-6 stonefly, and a small size-12 stonefly. Yes, Randy was planning on fishing three different stoneflies on one setup. His fly selection was good, all three of them legitimate flies I had seen catch plenty of fish. But the next thing he did really got me scratching my head.

Next, Randy attached a micro indicator about the size of a nickel. His fly selection was solid, but I instantly expected that this indicator couldn't hold up three heavy flies. But I kept my mouth shut. I had been given specific instructions and didn't want to challenge the expert's methods.

With Brian's rod rigged and ready, I put the boat into the mighty Snake. Off we pushed for a fun day of adventure and catching fish.

The first fishable spot of the day was 100 yards below the boat launch. Brian and Randy stood up and got ready for their first casts. Both of them knew what they were doing, so there were no casting lessons that morning.

Brian made a nice cast into the obvious drop-off below the gravel bar. His indicator settled nicely on the bubbly water. Then Randy made his first cast into the same green shelf. Within seconds, Randy's little neon-yellow indicator was sinking below the water. There it was, visible about two feet below the surface. Randy lifted his fly line to get the indicator back on the surface. Once the indicator was back on top, Randy gave his line some slack to start his drift. But as soon as his line had the extra slack, his indicator began to sink again.

After drifting about 30 feet, Brian hooked a beautiful rainbow trout. Randy acknowledged the catch with a large smile, and then continued to manipulate his line, trying to get the indicator to float the three heavy stoneflies. Brian managed to land the nice rainbow.

Brian cast again and instantly got bit by an acrobatic brown trout. To his credit, Randy quickly moved his line away from Brian's fish, then cast further behind the boat. Within moments, Randy's indicator was sinking several feet into the water. Once again, Brian landed his fish.

For the next half hour, Brian caught a handful more fish… but Randy couldn't get a bite. He was showing signs of growing frustration as his friend landed fish after fish after fish. Randy pulled his line in and changed one of his flies to a heavy San Juan Worm. Casting back out, we all watched as the little neon indicator instantly started to sink.

I knew why Randy wasn't catching any fish. I was surprised by his seeming lack of awareness of the situation. I figured, if he's owned a fly shop for 30 years, he surely knows the basics of indicator nymphing? Indicator fishing is relatively easy, something most novice fly anglers understand; it's basically glorified bobber fishing. I've never seen a conventional bobber fisherman use a sinking bobber. Doesn't that defeat the purpose? The whole point of a bobber is to float. When it floats, you can see it move uncharacteristically when a fish grabs something on your line below. But, then again, maybe my expert client knew something I didn't.

Trying to make sense of it, I turned around and asked Randy, "How do you know when a fish eats your fly?"

"What do you mean?" Randy asked.

"You're indicator fishing, but your indicator is constantly two to three feet under the water. I thought the point of the indicator was to have it float, so you can detect a strike," I explained.

"Ryan, I've been a fly shop owner for thirty years. This is how I wanna do it," Randy responded.

"Well, sure, Randy, that's great – but you didn't answer my question. How do you know when a fish eats your fly? With your indicator already submerged under the water?" I asked politely, truly wondering.

Randy looked at me intently.

"You know what?" he said. "I think I'm done fishing for the day."

"Wait, what? What do you mean, done for the day? Do you want a break?" I asked, kind of shocked. "Or do you want me to row to the takeout? We've been fishing less than an hour. I don't get it."

I turned back to Brian in the front and asked him, "Do you wanna go home too?"

Brian shook his head calmly. "I wanna keep fishing," he said. "This has been a great start. If we keep catching fish at this pace, I'll have one of the best fishing trips of my life."

So I turned back to Randy.

"Randy, sorry if I said something to offend you. I was just asking a question to understand your method of fishing. I like learning different styles of fly fishing, and I have never seen anyone fish a sinking indicator. I was just hoping to get your perspective on the method."

Randy, now obviously upset, shot back, "Ryan, I have owned a fly shop longer than you have been alive. I am an expert trout fisherman. I don't need some young guide asking me about my rigging methods!"

"I apologize for asking about your methods," I said. "I didn't realize my question would be upsetting. I am really sorry, Randy. I feel kinda stuck now. It's obvious you wanna go home, but your friend is catching a bunch of fish and having a blast. Brian wants to stay, and you don't. I'm not sure what to do here."

"That's fine. I'll just sit in the back and go for a ride," Randy said with an annoyed look on his face. "You just guide Brian, and I'll hang out and watch all of this beautiful trout water float past me."

"All right, if that's what you wanna do, I'm taking you for your word," I replied.

My full attention back on Brian, he was no longer sharing any of the runs with Randy and the fishing kept getting better and better for him. Cast after cast resulted in beautiful rainbow, brown, and cutthroat trout. The net was getting lots of action; Brian was smiling from ear to ear.

As the day went on, the sun popped out of the clouds,

shining brightly on the water and warming up the air. We approached a famous riffle, and, aha! the first glistening noses of the year showed themselves.

"Brian, look down there!" I called excitedly. "Do you see those rising fish in the middle of the riffle?"

Bran squinted his eyes as he looked downriver.

"Yeah! I see them," he said. "That's awesome! Does this mean we get to fish *dry flies*?"

"Yeah, man! You're gettin' the first day of dry-fly fishing this year!" I said excitedly. "I've been waiting weeks for this!"

As we watched the trout rise, Brian said, "One thing you gotta know, Ryan, I've never cast a dry fly."

"Really?! You've fished all over the world – you've never thrown a dry?" I asked. I couldn't believe it.

"Most of the destination fishing I've done for trout has always been fishing indicators or streamers," Brian explained. "The dry-fly game has always eluded me."

"Wow, man, that's surprising. But I'm excited to teach you," I said. "You've already landed a ton of fish today, so this is just the cherry on top!"

I spent the next 20 minutes teaching Brian how to cast and fish a dry fly, careful not to cast over our target fish. I wanted Brian to have as many shots as possible with his first dry fly attempt.

He was already an accomplished angler, so it didn't take Brian long to master the cast and presentation. After a few minutes, we shifted our attention to the rising trout in the riffle.

Brian's first cast was well placed. Within several seconds, a fish rose to his fly. But Brian was struggling to see his small dry fly in the sun's glare; he didn't see the fish eat his fly.

"The fish ate it!" I shrieked. "Set! Set!"

"Sorry, Ryan, I didn't see that one," said Brian.

"Oh, no worries," I responded. "Cast back up there and try again. Let's get another one."

Brian made another good cast toward the top of the riffle, and another fish ate his fly. But, again, Brian failed to react to the eat.

"Set!" I yelled. "Set the hook! The fish ate it!"

Brian quickly brought the rod up to set the hook, but he was late. The fish had already let go of his fly.

Out of nowhere, Randy spoke up.

"Ryan, you are the worst f***ing fly fishing guide I have ever hired," he said. "You have no clue what you're doing."

I turned around to confront Randy.

"Yep, I definitely don't know what I'm doing," I said. "Those thirty trout Brian caught today were all luck. I can't believe how lucky I am! I got thirty fish to eat with my minimal knowledge! You know, one day I hope to own a fly shop and really become an expert. I can't wait to understand the ways of sinking indicators. Yeah, over the last ten years of guiding, I haven't learned anything. You know what? I'm actually blown away those trout are eating Brian's dry fly. Gosh, what a lucky guess at the fly selection. I am *really* feeling lucky today, Randy."

"You are a terrible teacher," Randy replied. "Brian has a pod of rising trout in front of him, and he can't catch one."

"You know what, Randy? I know you think you're the expert in this boat, but I actually know quite a bit about this sport too," I said. "I may not own a fly shop, but I've been fly fishing since I was twelve years old. The reason Brian didn't catch a fish in his first two casts is because he's battling the glare from the sun.

The fish have eaten his fly on both casts, but we have to figure out the glare. Brian is a good fisherman and he's gonna do great. Maybe if we could focus on the fishing rather than your ego, he might actually catch his first dry-fly fish."

Randy just glared at me and didn't say another word.

"Sorry about all that, Brian," I said. "Go ahead and make another cast up there."

Brian picked out his next target in the riffle and made another cast. The fly settled softly on the water and the trout sipped in his fly.

This time his rod shot up quickly, and Brian was on!

He fought the fish well and landed a beautiful 18-inch cutthroat. Brian smiled with satisfaction from catching his first trout on a dry fly. After releasing the fish, I looked over at Brian.

"Damn, Brian, that was really lucky," I said. "It was so lucky, betcha can't do that again."

Brian smirked and then proceeded to make another cast. Then, just like the cast before, another fish came up and gently ate his fly. He landed a second fish on a dry. Then a third. Brian ended up landing 13 fish on dry flies in about an hour.

After hooking every rising fish in that riffle, Brian and I agreed it was probably best to row to the takeout. As I rowed to the boat launch, I told Brian, "That was the luckiest session of dry-fly fishing I have ever experienced as a guide. I am so shocked those fish ate that dry fly you were using. You were on such a roll. Randy should take you to a casino tonight to go win big."

Brian laughed. "Yeah, I wish I had a better teacher for my first time. Glad it worked out anyway."

I nodded my head in agreement and laughed with him.

"Sorry about that. I really have a lot to learn," I said. "Maybe next time I'll have a few more teaching tools to help you more. You know, catching over 40 trout in a day is just sad. I'm sorry I didn't do a better job." Brian smirked.

Once we got off the water, Brian came over to me privately and apologized for Randy. He told me that was the best day of trout fishing he had ever experienced, and he was bummed his friend had dampered the experience.

On the other hand, Randy gave his own report to Sebastian. I got an earful from my beloved manager about not following orders to ignore Randy.

Sebastian and I were close, and he knew it wasn't my guiding skills that ruined things for Randy. Randy was a person who thought he knew everything. Somehow, though, he didn't know that bobbers are supposed to float.

FRUSTRATION

Let's be honest, fly fishing is frustrating.

No matter what kind of fly angler you are, undoubtedly there have been moments in your fly fishing journey you've wanted to walk away. Quit. Throw in the towel.

For lots of us anglers, the frustration starts with learning how to cast. What the hell is up with this Brad Pitt, shadow-casting bullshit? Why do we need videos from professionals teaching us the art of casting? What happened to tying on a lure, opening the bail, and slinging it out there? Fly fishing is just not that simple.

I often wonder if the challenge of fly fishing is what draws many anglers to it. The simplicity of just chucking something out there in hopes a fish will eat it is nice, but at times, monotonous. The beauty of fly fishing is that no one picks up a fly rod for the first time and casts well. It's all hard-earned. Fly casting is something you learn over time. You quickly learn that the 10 o'clock, 2 o'clock cast rarely works; actually, it really limits your ability to cast for distance. Good fly casters are beautiful to watch as their line dances back and forth through the air. But remember, when they first picked up the fly rod, it looked about as pretty as Gene Simmons in spandex.

Once an angler can cast, then comes fish behavior, types of insects, watching tide charts, and lots and lots of time and experience. See, there are lots of good casters on this planet, but good casting does not make a good fisherman. I once worked for a lodge that hired a professional caster, let's call him Todd, to give a two-day-long casting lesson to all the guides. The idea was that if we learned from a great caster, then we would have the tools to better educate our clients. In theory, it was a great idea.

Todd would film every guide's cast, then critique each one to help us become better. It was pretty funny watching all the guides' faces as Todd told them how bad their casts were. Trust me, poor Todd was not given much credit or taken seriously.

After two days of facing our many flaws, we invited Todd out for a half-day of streamer fishing. Something about handing Todd a 7-weight rod with a heavy streamer really messed with his perfect 10 and 2 cast. When casting large, heavy flies, opening up your casting stroke allows for more space for your rod to load and your fly to travel. And, if you're casting large, heavy flies, with your cast close to your body, you're in for it. You'll get hooked, crack your skull, or break a rod tip. Not good.

To no one's surprise, the 7-weight and heavy flies gave Todd a run for his money. The goal of fishing streamers in a large Western tailwater is to get your fly as close as possible to the bank and then quickly strip 5-6 times to see if anything will chase. Once you've stripped it ten feet off the bank, you cast again. You're literally pounding the banks. Well, Todd was having a hard time getting his fly to land close enough to the bank. River streamer fishing is a game of accuracy. Let's just say our professional caster was playing hand grenades instead of horse shoes.

We kept encouraging Todd to cast closer to the bank, but he could only get his fly about 4 feet away from every target we pointed out. Eventually his 10 and 2 cast bit him in the ass as he broke his rod tip and whacked himself in the back. Poor Todd gave himself quite a welt.

He sat down shaking his head in frustration. "You can forget everything I tried to teach you about casting. My cast is for the lawn, not chucking big streamers on large rivers. This is really hard," Todd grumbled.

Even guys who get paid to teach casting get frustrated. Fly fishing can be an amazingly rewarding sport, but it can also humble us all. Let's assume you're able to get past the frustrations of casting and actually start to master the fly cast. That in itself is a major victory, but it doesn't make you a great fisherman. There are so many different fly fishing techniques for different waters and fish that it seems nearly impossible to master them all. Sure, try to take on a new technique – the frustration bug is always lurking around the corner.

There will be days when the fish don't cooperate. You've cast every fly in the book and they keep refusing all of your offerings. Kinda like a toddler in need of a nap. Nothing you do will make the fish eat. Now you're stuck on the water yelling at the fish, "Will you just EAT MY FLY!!!" Sorry to break it to you, but you can yell all you want; it doesn't help the fishing one bit. On the other hand, showing the fish respect by giving them the first pour of each beer you drink is a totally different story. That absolutely works.

You want to talk about other frustrating aspects of our sport? Is there anything more frustrating than bad weather? There are days the weather absolutely nukes you. The wind, rain, and snow block you from approaching the fishing like you normally would. All the tricks in your bag are useless as the wind gusts in your face. You finally have the day off work, the tides are perfect, there are fish boiling everywhere, but you can't get to them because the damn wind blows every cast right back in your face.

A friend of mine saved up all of his disposable income to purchase a fishing trip to the flats of Belize. When he got there, a big storm rolled in with gusts of wind from 50-60mph. Sadly, the storm hunkered down on them, and they never left the beach all 7 days. They paid all that money to watch the rain fall, wind blow, and drink some really expensive drinks with froofy umbrellas. Of course, on their day of departure, the weather settled down and the sun came out to say goodbye with a smile.

Remember the moment you had that fish of a lifetime feeding right in front of you? It was as though you were at the Fly Fishing Film Tour, and the film was playing in high def slow motion before your very eyes: a massive fish in your crosshairs, you make a miracle cast, the fish moves over and aggressively inhales your fly, you set the hook too hard, and the fish breaks off. Now, in my opinion, that could be one of the most frustrating moments in all of fly fishing.

Fly fishing can be one of the most enjoyable sports, but like most things in life, there are still frustrating moments to push through. I will never forget the day I broke off the largest steelhead I ever hooked. I waited 25 years for that moment, with thousands and thousands of casts leading up to my first 20lb steelhead, and it was gone in an instant. I have witnessed countless clients go through countless frustrating fishing moments in my boat, but never have I seen someone so angry as this one day, wading the Fryingpan River, in Colorado.

My friend Mike and I had been enjoying a week-long fishing trip in the wonderful state of Colorado. We had bounced around to a handful of different rivers before ending up on the Fryingpan River for several days. The Fryingpan, or "the Pan" as locals call it, is home to lots of really large trout. Some of the trout on the Pan can grow to absolutely insane sizes. Every year, there are 10-plus pound trout landed from this small wadeable river in Colorado.

Mike and I had landed a handful of solid rainbows in the five-pound class, and we were having a great time doing it. The challenging, and often frustrating, part of fishing the Pan is that you have to fish micro flies to these fish. They're often caught with light tippet on midges with hooks in the 20-24 size range. It's hard enough to thread the flies on your tippet, let alone catch a 5-pound trout on it. After fishing there for two days, we had lost so many fish. They kept coming unhooked during the fight. And, we had broken off enough flies on our hooksets to make up a month of profit for the local fly shop. All of our losses were part of the challenge, fun, and frustration of fishing highly technical tailwaters with micro-sized flies.

Our last afternoon on the river, we decided to walk up to

a different fishing spot. As we walked along the tall towering bank overlooking the river, we noticed another angler intensely fishing behind a large rock. We stopped for a moment and peered into the water behind the rock.

"Oh my god, do you see the size of that fish, Mike? That thing is gigantic," I whispered.

"Wow, that thing is incredible! I thought it was a boulder under the water. Holy crap! That's the biggest trout I've ever seen!" Mike muttered.

We sat there in awe of that fish. Each of us was slightly jealous of our fellow angler down below. He made a perfect cast directly behind the boulder, lifted his line off the water, then watched his leader float by the fish. But cast after cast, there was no success. After about a dozen casts, he pulled his flies in, cut off a fly, opened up his fly box, carefully studied his fly box, picked out the next fly, and tied it on.

This progression of fly fishing stratergery continued for over an hour. Mike and I were intrigued by the angler's persistence. If I was in his spot, I would have signed a lease before I landed that beast. My beard would be four feet long and I would smell like the dirty streets of San Francisco. Then one day someone on the bank would yell down at me, "Hey! You know that fish is just a rock!"

Mike and I hung in there with this guy. Every 10 minutes, he would change his fly out. He tried adjusting the length of his leader, the amount of his split shot, everything a knowledgeable angler would try. Nothing was working. Yet every cast, he stayed focused. Finally, about the 20th fly change, Mike and I saw a flash of white, and the monster ate his fly.

The angler quickly swung his rod up and set the hook.

The trout rock made one massive head shake from right to left and freed the tiny little midge from its jaw.

In an instant, the fish of a lifetime was hooked... and unhooked.

Mike and I barely breathed. Our hands shot up in Halleluia victory, then quickly clutched our foreheads as we felt our fellow angler's pain.

The line loosened, and the angler's head sunk to his chest. His whole body went limp as he stared down into the water. The current swung his fly line and rod down below him. There before us was a broken fly fisherman. Defeated. Hours and hours spent on this fish with such a terrible end.

Life returned to his body. He pulled off his hat and fiercely slapped the water with it. He screamed every cuss word in the book. Now it was harder to watch, as the angler cycled through waves of grief. Finally in one last moment of rage, he aggressively stormed out of the river and yelled, "I HATE THIS F***ING SPORT!"

Now the frustrated angler gazed upon his rod with fire in his eyes. He held the rod high above his head, then slammed it over his knee. It snapped in two. He looked at the broken pieces for a moment, then chucked the whole kit and caboodle out into the river. He stomped off down the trail and yelled one last time.

"Eat THAT, trout!"

Some level of frustration at some point of fly fishing is inevitable. The sport is too complex to have everything under control. Maybe it's never happened to you – you just love being out on the water, enjoying the fish and fresh air, and not being at work. Well, if you fish long enough, I believe the frustration

bug will come for you. I recommend a deep breath, or a walk...
but keep your fishing rod intact. Break a stick instead.

CHIEF ROW-A-LOT

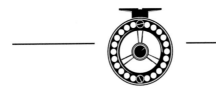

As with most things in this world, our nation's schools are constantly evolving. When it comes to education, I understand that our schools have to elevate their processes to keep up with the times. I have the privilege of being a father to two wonderful school-aged girls, and I've noticed some changes in education since my school days. For anyone who hasn't experienced the "modern" methods, I speculate you might be surprised. Let's take math, for example. Simple addition problems like 100+150 = 250 look a lot different in textbooks these days.

I was hanging out at my friend's house one day when his son came into the room asking for some help with his homework. He was a freshman in high school at the time, taking basic algebra, and he was trying to solve a math problem. At the table were three grown men, all with undergraduate business degrees and MBA's. So, educated. The intelligence level among the group was…decent enough. We could tell this kid the answer, we could show him how to come up with the answer, but we were wrong. We were using old problem-solving methods that are no longer accepted in his class. Can you believe that? We work the problem, show the work, find the correct answer, and it's considered wrong because it's the old way. Talk about a head scratcher.

The educational changes are not only in math; they seem to be across all the subjects. Thankfully, the Alphabet Song we learned as toddlers is still safe for the moment. Think about how history books are constantly being rewritten. The history our grandparents, parents, and our own generation was taught is now being changed by academia. Kids are learning a lot less about our past. I believe there is a massive lack of knowledge about our country's history.

I once had a guide trip on the Snake River in Idaho with two college students that really opened my eyes to the lack of historical knowledge among this generation. Scott was 20 years old, a sophomore at the University of Tennessee; Kyle was 21, a junior at the University of Alabama (Roll Tide). They had been friends since childhood and attended high school together. Together with their dads, the boys had fished a lot of the famous rivers in the south, but they had never been to the Rockies. Scott and Kyle were excited to have this special fishing trip in the Wild West, including three days in my boat without any parental figures. We had lots of fun conversations about college, SEC football, frat parties, and chasing girls.

Scott and Kyle had heard great stories about fishing the canyon stretch of the South Fork, famous for its staggering natural beauty. I have fished for trout all over the West, and it's one of the prettiest floats I've seen. The South Fork has a lot of beautiful sections, but none as breathtaking as the canyon, with its massive cliff walls shooting thousands of feet straight up from the water. Mile after mile, around every corner, is another postcard view.

One of my favorite parts of fishing the canyon is its vastness, how small it makes me feel. Everything around us is large, from the wide river to the massive cliffs to the tall cottonwoods. As we floated from spot to spot, Kyle and Scott were in quiet awe of the beauty that surrounded them. Eventually, Scott broke the silence.

"Ryan, I have a question for you," he said. "Do you guys still have Indians tribes living on the river?"

As the water slapped my oars, I had to pause to process the question. Did this guy really just ask me if there are Indians living on the river? This is an educated guy who should know about the history of this country and Native Americans. Did he sleep through all of this in high school history class? Suddenly, a light bulb went on. "This could be really fun," I thought.

"Actually, as a matter of fact, Scott, we have the last active Snake River Indian tribe still living on the river," I replied. "Oftentimes, when we come around this large bend in the river, the chief of the tribe, with his large headdress of bald eagle feathers, is sitting on his horse overlooking the lands. He just sits up there peacefully watching all of the drift boats and fly fishers float down the river. The best part is the grizzly bear claw necklace he wears around his neck."

"Really? That's so cool. Is there a chance we may see him up there?" Scott asked.

"Maybe, if we're really lucky," I replied. "We only see the chief a few times a week."

"Wow, man. That's awesome," said Kyle, chiming in. "I hope we get to see him."

"Yeah, it's pretty special when that happens," I said. "But there is one thing the two of you need to know: We have made a peace treaty with the tribe. Two miles downriver from here, we're not allowed to fish. The tribe has a three-mile no-fishing zone to respect the resources near their camps. We have to quietly float by their camp of tepees and not aggravate the native people. So, just as a heads up, we'll have to take a break soon. Please don't take any pictures, and respect their privacy."

"Ryan, this is going to be awesome. I can't believe I'm going to see Snake River Indians living in their natural environment," Scott said. "My history professor is going to freak out when I tell him this."

"Yep, he sure is," I replied with a smile.

We continued our fishing journey downriver, bouncing back and forth from one bank to the other. The consistent action of catching trout on dry flies kept the two boys interested and engaged. They were having a great time on their first trip to the Snake River.

"Okay, guys," I said after we finished the last good fishable bank. "Get ready to see the chief coming up around the next bend."

I pointed to the top of the cliff, and both looked in the same direction. "Look around," I said with a smirk. "I don't see him up there today. Sometimes he is in different spots around the cliff, so keep your eyes peeled up there."

"I don't see him, Ryan," Kyle said.

"Yeah, I don't either," I replied. "I guess we're unlucky today. Alright, let's get back to fishing."

Scott and Kyle turned their attention back to the bank and started casting in hopes of raising another trout. We fished for another hour, then started to approach the closed Indian fishing zone.

"Okay, guys, it's time to reel them up," I said. "We're getting dangerously close to the edge of the closed fishing zone. I need you to reel your lines in, hook up your fly, sit down, and be extremely quiet. If you want to talk, we need to do that quietly. If we were to be confronted by any of the Indian warriors, please don't say anything and let me take care of it."

Scott and Kyle nodded their heads in agreement as they slowly sat down. They reeled in their lines and put their rods away.

As we sat there, floating down the river, I said, "Keep an eye out. You never know when they are watching you. The Indian camp is just around the next corner, way back in this big grove of cottonwood trees. Please, try to be quiet."

Both had their heads on a swivel, scanning every shady spot in the trees. As we continued to float down the river, you could tell the excitement of seeing the camp was starting to build.

As we floated around the corner, I let out a big yell. "No! No!"

"What's wrong, Ryan?," Kyle asked.

"Their camp is gone. They must have moved it in the last couple of days. That could only mean one thing: Someone broke the no-fishing treaty. This is bad, guys. Really, really, bad. This means we might not ever be able to fish this river again."

"Oh, no. That really sucks," replied Scott.

Just as the words came out of Scott's mouth, I couldn't

take it anymore. I started laughing out loud with a big, deep belly laugh.

"What's so funny?" Kyle asked.

"You guys can't really believe all that I just told you over the last hour, right?" I replied. "There are no Indians living on the river. There is no chief that overlooks the river. Nor was there a peace treaty made to fish the river."

"Wait, so you just made all of that up?" Scott asked.

"One hundred percent of it," I said. "I was just trying to be funny and make you guys laugh. Then, you didn't laugh and you started asking questions about my fictional story. I began to wonder how long I could make the story last. At some point I assumed you would catch on. I mean, you are both educated guys going to college. Did you not pay attention in history class?"

Scott and Kyle started laughing and shaking their heads in disbelief. Kyle then looked at Scott and said, "We're two idiots for believing Ryan's story."

Scott, looking out toward the river bank, sarcastically replied, "Alright, Chief Row-a-Lot, you got us on that one. You're one funny guy. Thanks for giving us a history lesson on the Wild West. Can we get back to fishing now?"

"Absolutely, Chief Catch-a-Lot-of-Fish," I said with a huge smile on my face.

AAARRR!!!

Most of my short stories focus on my clients. As a guide, the people I hang out with are usually the most interesting and hence entertaining part of my profession. For this chapter, however, we will shift our attention to a once-in-a-lifetime interaction with a very peculiar cutthroat trout.

The day I encountered this fish started off no different than any other day on the job. I walked into the fly shop that morning and met my client for the day. Josh was in his mid-thirties and from New Jersey. He had the young, modern, fly fishing look down pat, with a trimmed salt-and-pepper beard, flat-billed hat, high-end sunglasses, a buff around his neck, quick-dry shorts, and flip flops. His raccoon eyes were indicative of the two-week fly fishing vacation through the Rockies he was in the midst of. He had already fished the famous waters of Montana – the

Madison, Beaverhead, and Big Hole, to name a few – and now he was making his way through eastern Idaho. He had stopped at the legendary Henry's Fork of the Snake, and he wanted to give the South Fork a try before making his way into Wyoming.

The fishing that morning started off slowly. We were in that part of the summer when the bite doesn't pick up until after lunch, when the pale morning dun mayflies start to hatch. Josh fished a hopper-dropper rig, and as the morning progressed, he caught a handful of nice rainbows, browns, and cutthroats on the bead-head nymph floating below his dry fly.

We enjoyed a nice lunch on one of my favorite riffles as we waited for the PMD hatch to start. As we ate our sandwiches and chips, our eyes were trained on the water, looking for the first sign of life. After a while, a beautiful and delicate little mayfly lifted off the water; then a second, a third, and a fourth. Within minutes, hundreds of bugs were emerging from the soft riffle.

It didn't take long for the fish to notice, and then suddenly there were glistening noses sipping in every little meal. I often think of mayflies like french fries from a burger joint. The stoneflies and hoppers are the burgers—the main course—but the small mayflies are like fries floating down the river. If you eat too many french fries, or mayflies in this case, you'll feel full.

Josh caught a handful of nice fish in the riffle on a small, size-18 PMD emerger. After we wore out our welcome and the trout were no longer willing to play, we moved downriver. We had floated about another mile when I spotted a large cutthroat feeding in the foam behind a scraggly bush. I quickly spun the boat around and set Josh up for an upstream cast.

He pulled some line off his reel and made a beautiful and delicate cast to the current seam coming off the edge of the bush. The fly landed in the perfect spot. We had no doubt the fish would come up and slurp in his emerger. Perfect casts are rare on the water, but this was one of them.

The fly settled onto the pillowy, foamy water and danced like a tiny ballerina on the tips of her toes. It slowly floated toward the cutthroat, but our expectations were met with disappointment. The cutty paid no attention to Josh's fly and continued to feed on the natural PMDs floating by.

I told Josh to put a second cast in the exact same spot. Just like before, he made a textbook presentation. But again, there was no interest from the fish, which instead continued to gluttonously eat every PMD in sight. A third and fourth cast brought the same results. Nothing. Nada. The fish was feeding aggressively all right, but it didn't like the fly Josh was using. So I decided to tie on a different PMD pattern I used frequently. Josh made another amazing cast, and once again there was no reaction from the fish.

"What the hell's going on?" I asked. "Cutthroats are supposed to be easy to catch on dry flies."

Josh made a few more casts with no luck. For some reason, this fish wasn't into regular french fries. I wondered if I should go with garlic parmesan, truffle oil, or maybe even sweet potato curly fries.

"Hey, pass me your fly. I wanna try a sneaky pattern," I said to Josh. I didn't use this one often, but it had worked well on picky fish in the past.

Josh got back into position and threw an absolute bull's eye cast into the feeding zone. Nothing happened. Now I was officially irritated with this fish. No doubt it was pillaging the innocent village of mayflies near its foamy resting place. I just could not figure out its favorite recipe. I had seen this scenario hundreds of times, and I know how to catch these fish, so I was determined to make it happen for Josh. After all, he had been dropping pinpoint casts into the feeding zone. He deserved it.

Then, oddly, Josh made an errant cast that landed three feet to the left of the fish. In my mind, there was a zero percent chance the cast would work. Before I could tell Josh to recast, the cutthroat swam over and slurped in Josh's floating french fry. He quickly and firmly set the hook on a monster 24-inch cutthroat.

"Holy shit! How did *that* cast work?" I said. "No offense, man, but that cast was terrible! Nothing about that makes sense. I've seen thousands of trout rise to dry flies, and that should not have happened!"

We followed the fish out to the middle of the river. Josh fought it well, slowly tiring it out. I scooped that beautiful, gold-and-orange slab into the net where I noticed something very peculiar about this fish: It was missing its right eye! The fish had been swimming slightly to the left of the current seam, so every time Josh made a perfect cast, the fly would slowly float down the current seam completely unseen by the trout. Finally, when the fly landed way to the *left*, the one-eyed fish actually had a chance to see it!

It's wise to keep trying new patterns when we're trying to figure out what the fish are feeding on, and by all means, keep making great presentations, too. But life – and fish – are weirdly unpredictable.

Sometimes the most perfect protocols go right out the window, like when you're dealing with a pirate fish. "Got it, matey? Aaarrrr!!!"

CLASS IS IN SESSION

As we journey through life's twists and turns, we are constantly learning. An especially difficult situation, problem, new skill, or interaction can really make it apparent- okay, I'm learning something here, whether I want to or not!

The same is true for fishing. When we're out on the water, we are constantly learning. For example, which flies tend to catch more fish. Generally speaking, the best-looking fly in the bin isn't always The One. Often the simple and subdued patterns, the less expensive flies, are more productive.

We also learn bigger, more important lessons out there fishing, like, don't wade across the turbulent river to get to a "sexy"-looking fishing spot on the other side. Drowning is not worth a fish- any fish. Only in our imaginations are the fish on the unreachable side of the river always bigger. Be realistic. That's not true, and drowning sucks.

I'm always learning as a fly fishing guide. How to interact more effectively with clients, new fishing techniques, fish behavior, tying knots…conditions are always changing and challenging me to learn more. For example, when my clients are breaking off a lot of fish, I'm wondering, "Maybe I should be doing more than three twists on my clinch knots?"

One memorable learning opportunity as a guide took place in my late 20's. It was one of those lessons that sticks with you the rest of your life.

I was trout fishing on the upper Green River outside Pinedale, Wyoming, a quick two-day fishing trip with my dad. We planned one day wading the river on our own, then the second day would be a guided drift boat trip. I was excited to fish with my dad, and have someone else guide us. I'm usually the guide, and usually rowing; any day stepping into the boat as a fisherman is a real treat.

The first day, my dad and I tromped around the river catching lots of trout on hopper dropper rigs. It was early August in central Wyoming, so the hoppers were just getting active. The trout seemed happy to welcome their mid-summer treats back to the river banks. When a slight wind blew, a cloud of hoppers would lose their bearings and end up landing in the water. There, as the hopper vigorously kicked its legs to swim to safety, a trout would aggressively rise and smash the large, summer delicacy.

Ah, summer! The fishing was good. Most riffles and soft water pockets behind rocks held a handful of trout, mostly in the normal 12"-16" range. A few pushed 18" but nothing nearly big enough to bother pulling out a camera. I was all about hanging with my dad, waving a rod around, enjoying the beauty of summer. By all accounts, it was a great day. We went to bed content. But I was super excited for our guide trip the next day.

Day two, we met our guide at the local fly shop. He was a really nice guy who had been guiding for several years. He was in his early thirties with a strong body, a warm smile, and like most guides had a large racoon-like sunglass tan on his face. We drove to the river talking about the day that lay ahead of us – normal small talk about the current fishing conditions, the progression of the summer's hatches, then eventually a crazy story from earlier that week.

As we closed in on the river, I asked, "What techniques will we use today?"

"We're gonna fish hopper dropper rigs, targeting the undercut banks and riffles, for rainbows and browns."

That's what I figured, but I wanted to double check. He was describing the same method we had used the day before, and it worked well. Who doesn't enjoy casting hoppers at a bank and watching trout engulf them? It made sense to rinse and repeat.

Well, I was in need of a change. I thought, if I went along with the guide's methods, I would catch a bunch of fish, but most of them would look like yesterday's. I was hoping to target the larger fish, so I said, "Yeah, yesterday I fished a hopper dropper rig all day, and caught a ton. I was hoping I could try fishing streamers today, see if I can dredge up a big one. Would that be okay with you?"

"Of course, man. You do need to know, there will be clear bright skies today. That doesn't always make for the best streamer fishing. My guess is you'll only have two eats all day. The fish that eat streamers are gonna be on the larger side, but you're gonna have to fish hard to get your bites."

"Yeah, I totally expect that. I'm willing to fish hard. I got my fill of catching fish yesterday. I'm hoping to find something bigger today."

"Let's do it. I love when clients wanna fish streamers. Nothing better than heading out on the river, hunting for river monsters."

I was thankful our guide was willing to switch his fishing methods. At the end of the day, if I didn't catch anything, the streamer call would lie 100 percent on my shoulders, but I was okay with that. I believed in my own skill and fishing prowess to make up for the lack of opportunities with less-than-ideal streamer weather conditions.

We arrived at the river and our guide got the boat prepped for the day.

"Darrel, do you wanna fish streamers too?"

"Nah, I think I'll stick with your hopper dropper rig. One thing I've learned over many years of hiring guides, is to do what they suggest. I'm not gonna follow my son on a rogue mission, trying to find a random monster fish in bad conditions."

We all laughed at my dad's comment. The guide proceeded to pick his favorite hopper dropper patterns for the day. After he had my dad rigged up, he turned his attention to my rod.

"Ryan, do you have a preference on streamers?"

"No, not really. You're the one fishing this river all the time. Whatever you wanna tie on will work for me."

He dug into his large boat bag. It was full of fishing gear. In true Mary Poppins fashion, he reached deeper and deeper and deeper into the bag, making it clear he hadn't fished any streamers for quite some time. First came the hopper dry fly box, then the large stonefly dry box, then the small dries box, and then came the multitude of nymph boxes. As the mountain of fly boxes grew on his tailgate, he finally found the box of streamers– very much rested from disuse in the bottom of his bag.

He opened the streamer box, peering into the furry, overflowing collection of flies. He rubbed his chin while he meditated over his selection. What would today's weapon be? Slowly and methodically, he touched each one, deep in deliberation.

"Okay. I think you should fish this gray over white rabbit strip streamer. I've caught more big fish on this streamer than any other in my box. Plus, with the bright sunshine, every fish in the river is gonna see this fly."

"Sounds good. I like the looks of that fly. For the current conditions, I think you made a great choice," I responded.

He put away his impressive collection of flies and launched the boat into the water. We were off.

Our guide put my dad in the front of the boat with the hopper dropper rig. I was in the back with the streamer rod. Flies with a delicate presentation, the dry fly in this situation, are better fished ahead of the large bomb of a streamer slapping the water over and over.

I was excited for another day of fishing with my dad, but I was ecstatic to be off the oars. To be honest, I didn't really care about catching anything that day. I wanted to have some fun, drink a couple beers, enjoy someone else rowing the boat for once, and maybe get a grab on a streamer.

As we started our float down the river, our guide turned to me in the back and said, "Now you need to be aware of how fish eat streamers on this river. This is not your normal river, where they slam your fly with a kill eat. Often on this river, the fish will barely pick up your fly. All you feel is a small tap, tap."

He reached over to my shirt and pinched the sleeve. "The grab won't be much more than this." Two quick, soft tugs on my sleeve showed me how it would feel.

"Gotcha," I nodded. I'd been fishing streamers for trout my entire life, and never once had the eat been subtle. A subtle streamer eat didn't exist in my book. A streamer mimics another fish, or a sculpin, or a leech, that kind of thing. These critters are swimming away quickly from the predatorial trout, so the trout only have one option: an aggressive eat. And the hostile eats are the true beauty and fun of fishing a streamer.

As our morning progressed, my dad caught a bunch of regular-sized trout, much like he had the day before. Every fishy spot gave him another one. Some were on the hopper, but most were on the dropper nymph down below. After several hours went by, my dad had easily landed twenty trout. He was cheerfully entertained.

Our guide released the latest of my dad's trout then gingerly asked me, "You sure you're okay with that streamer? You haven't had any eats or followers all morning."

"I'm good, man. I know what I signed up for. I'm only after one or two fish today. Don't sweat me not catching anything – I wanna hunt the big ones."

"All right, well, keep swingin' for the fences," he cheered mildly.

The hours rolled on by. Eventually we pulled into this really deep run full of large boulders. I couldn't see the bottom through my polarized glasses. I casted my fly over the big rocks and threw a huge stack mend into my line to allow the fly to sink. I let this one soak longer, hoping my fly would get down deep. While I waited for my fly to sink, I switched my attention to my dad fishing.

In a semi-mesmerized state, watching my dad cast back and forth, I felt a fish hammer my streamer so hard it almost pulled the rod out of my hand. It was the craziest thing; I wasn't stripping the fly or making it move in any way. Somewhere in the depths of the run, the fish swam over so fast and hard to engulf the streamer, it literally set the hook on itself.

"Whoa! Damn, that was a hard eat!" I said enthusiastically.

I quickly brought the rod tip up to fight the fish. It made a thrashing jump out of the water. There before us was a slab of a rainbow, white and gray streamer hanging out the side of its mouth.

After a brief and intense fight, I landed the beautiful and thick 24-inch buck rainbow. The trout was in the five-to-six-pound class with a medium-sized kype and a beautiful crimson-pink stripe running down its thick side. That grab is still the best freshwater streamer eat I've ever felt. Like the fish hadn't eaten for a month and suddenly a T-bone steak appeared on his plate. That streamer was devoured.

There was no soft tap, tap to that streamer grab. That was a kill eat.

"Now remember, not all eats are gonna be like that. The next grab could be really subtle."

"Yeah, man. I'm ready for it," I replied. But on the inside, I was thinking, "How much streamer fishing does this guide do?" After what I had just experienced, I wasn't completely buying his prediction. Sure, there's a big variation in streamer eats, but subtle? I've never had a subtle streamer eat.

The day was getting late, my dad's face was growing tired from all the success smiling, and I was stoked on my big catch. If that wasn't enough, we headed into this really incredible-looking run, starting with a perfect drop off, then a gradually sloped riffle. The riffle would get deeper and deeper, eventually dumping into this major seam line flowing directly along a deep, dark, undercut bank. Perfect streamer water.

My dad and I both fished through the heart of the run. No luck. Then we got to the tail out of the run, where it shallows up. Tail outs are generally better for dry flies and swinging soft hackles, so I stripped in half my line and did a roll cast behind the boat. I would just wait for the next good streamer spot.

With my fly dragging along the bottom of the shallow tailout behind us, waiting patiently in non-fish mode, my focus turned back to my dad. I felt a small tap, tap. I thought of the shallow water and made a blind roll cast to keep my fly from getting stuck in the rocks.

Quickly I felt another soft tap, tap.

"What the hell? My fly hasn't even had enough time to sink to the bottom yet," I thought.

I turned my whole self around to investigate. There was the largest brown trout I have ever seen. And it was swimming downriver, toward the boat, *with my streamer in its mouth.*

"Oh my god!" I hollered.

Completely lost in the moment, with my line only pinched under my stripping finger, not even in my left hand, I did a rod set as hard as I could, throwing the rod tip high up in the air.

The massive brown trout felt the tension on the line and opened its mouth to let the fly go. With the entire universe in slow motion, I watched that fish dump my streamer and make a U-turn to head home.

"Nooooo! Damn it! Shit! Biggest brown of my life! I can't believe that just happened. I wasn't even fishing!" I cried.

"How big did it look?" our guide asked.

"Over 30 inches, easy. My biggest trout was a 27-inch brown. It was significantly bigger than that."

"Did it eat hard?" he asked me.

"Nope. It was subtle, just like you said..."

"Weird how these fish do that," he replied. "I've never seen subtle streamer eats anywhere else, just here," he said with a smirk. I deserved it.

We learn a lot of lessons while fly fishing. Some of them are even about fishing. The best ones will correct our poor, sorry selves when we haven't learned our lesson yet. Then all we can do is hope it takes, so we don't have to learn it again. I haven't had a soft streamer take since that day behind the boat, but you better believe I set the hook properly every time I feel that tap, tap. And I listen to my guide.

COMPETITION

Get a bunch of men together, whether at a workplace, a bar, or a backyard barbecue, it's pretty natural to see some kind of one-upmanship. Pride loves to play peek-a-boo, and all that testosterone pulls us down to our bare instincts. Sometimes there's even chest beating.

This male tendency to compete shows up on the water too. I have two longtime clients who start every fishing day with some friendly wagering. Their competition, which includes four separate bets of $10 each, starts with the first cast and ends on the last. Categories include:

First fish

Largest fish

Most fish

Last fish

The competition motivates them to fish harder and stay focused throughout the day. It's a fun game between friends, and only once has one of them walked away with $40 in his pocket. This, of course, led to much dancing and gloating by the victor.

In my opinion, there's nothing wrong with a little friendly competition. Many of us enjoy a good game of cards, a board game, or a bet on our favorite sports team. The issue is when friendly competition morphs into something darker and more intense. That's when our knuckle-dragging ways take over and we're tempted to show up our fellow man. The ego kicks level-headed, logical thought to the curb, and the new goal is simply domination.

I see it a lot on the river. Most of the time I just laugh it off, but one morning, while guiding in Idaho, another guide really got under my skin.

The day started like any other. I met my clients, we picked out some flies, loaded the cooler, and headed down the road to the boat launch. We had a pleasant conversation about where they were from, how long they had been fly fishing, and what brought them to the South Fork of the Snake River.

When we got to the launch, we were greeted by a long line of trucks and drift boats. This particular launch was literally a dirt slide off the side of the road. Only one boat could launch at a time, and it was never a quick process.

This was no kids' slide at the park. This was a steep 100 foot grade to the river's edge. We'd back the trailer to the drop-off, then slowly crank the boat onto the ground. Once the drift boat was off the trailer, we would grab the front of the boat, push off, and attempt to ride the boat to the river's edge like a rodeo bull. Most of the time, the guide would make it the full eight seconds, but occasionally, we'd see one get bucked off, his boat shooting out into the river with no one in it. That was never a swim I wanted to take. Over the years, a handful of boats have been lost at this particular launch.

As I waited in line for my turn to ride the drift boat bull, my clients and I took our time putting together the rods, rigging flies, and getting the boat prepped for the day. After about 15 minutes, we were finally next in line to slide my boat off the edge. The guide ahead of us was walking back from parking his truck when he stopped to chat.

"I see from your license plate you're from California," he said.

"Yes, sir," I replied.

He looked off into the distance as if deep in contemplation, then looked back at me.

"Huh, I didn't know California guides knew how to catch fish," he said. "Everyone I've known from California was a terrible fisherman."

I took his jab and just smiled back.

"I know a few tricks," I said. "Maybe not as many as you, but I'm confident I can get the job done."

He looked over at my clients.

"Sorry you guys are stuck with a guide from California," he told them. "I hope the lodge will refund your money. Good luck catching anything today."

He chuckled as he sauntered off. I glanced at my clients. Their faces both registered the shock, surely at the guide's lack of respect.

"Don't worry about that guy," I told them calmly. "That was really unnecessary. You guys have nothing to be worried about. I'm really good at guiding and fishing this river. You're in great hands."

However, after successfully launching my boat down the slide, I felt my deep, dark beast mode awaken on the walk back to the river. And I didn't stop it.

"How dare he come over here and try to show me up like that!" I thought to myself. *"What a TOOL! Just because I'm from California doesn't mean I'm a bad guide. So what if we don't have the famous waters of the Rockies? We still have some bad ass fly fishing. What does he know about California, anyway? We may have our issues, but so do these idiots."*

Then I went from beast mode to monster mode.

"Screw that guy," my internal dialog continued. *"Who does he think he is?! I think what he needs is a good lesson. He needs to know that a guide from California can row circles around his ass."*

My heart raced, my breath was short, and my pace quickened as I made my way down to my boat and clients. I remembered my real job, took a deep breath and smiled.

"Hey, guys, if it's all right with you, I'm gonna row for a while to catch up with my new boat launch buddy," I told my clients. "I feel like I need to show him a few things. I wanna give him an education on California guides."

They both laughed.

"That sounds like fun," one of them said. "I'd love to put that dude in his place."

I appreciated their willingness to go along with the twisted competition I had created in my own beastly pride. As I rowed downriver, I could see him just half a mile ahead of us. I watched his moves, gathering data on the types of water he liked to fish. I knew the South Fork like the back of my hand after guiding there for five seasons, and I made a game plan as I watched him skip several good spots.

The guide rowed to a famous bank and had his clients cast toward the grassy edge. It was definitely a good spot, but what the guide didn't know is the trout preferred the deep gravel edge. He literally had his clients fishing the wrong side of the boat.

I rowed up to within about 30 feet of the guide's boat and instructed my clients to stand up.

"I know it looks like we should be fishing the bank, but the other side is way better," I told them. "Both of you cast to the left, about 20 to 25 feet off the boat."

They both made great casts, and their flies fell softly to the water. As their drifts began, the angler in the bow had a nice brown trout rise up and engulf his fly. He set the hook and the fight was on. As soon as he hooked the fish, I loudly yelled, "Fish on! That's a good one!"

The other guide looked over his shoulder to see us fishing right behind him. He had a front row seat to my client landing the brown trout. We quickly released it so he could make another cast. Within seconds, he hooked another brown, and once again I yelled, "Fish on! You got another one!"

The guide looked over his shoulder again to watch us land the fish. Now he began to row downriver.

Watching his every move, I said to my clients, "Why don't you guys take a seat. We're gonna row for a while. I'm not gonna let this guy run away."

The guide rowed another mile downriver, passing lots of good water as he tried to get away. I kept pushing on the oars with no intention of stopping until he did. After about 15 minutes of rowing, he decided to try another bank. This time he made the mistake of fishing the left bank when the right bank was much more productive. So, rather than fish behind him, I positioned my boat directly across the river from him.

My clients stood up and began to fish. Within five casts, one of them had hooked another trout.

"FISH ON!" I yelled over my shoulder.

Then, within a matter of seconds, my other client hooked a fish. "DOUBLE!" I yelled even louder.

The guide looked over his shoulder again. We locked eyes. I gave him a nod, and he turned his attention back to his clients.

We landed the two trout. Then without a pause, I rowed hard across the river to get directly behind the other guide, literally 20 feet from his boat. My clients casted, and one of them hooked a nice trout right behind his boat.

"You got another one!" I yelled. "You're on fire!"

It was obvious our new friend was getting frustrated. Maybe he just needed some "space." Again he aggressively rowed down the river.

"Looks like we're going for another row," I told my clients.

Well acquainted with the drill by now, they dutifully sat down and egged me on. We would spend the next four hours chasing the other guide down the river. When he fished, we fished. When he rowed, I rowed. The entire morning, he was never more than 50 yards in front of me. His clients caught a handful of fish, but we caught five fish for every one they caught. He stopped for lunch around 1pm, and I stopped for lunch just behind him.

After lunch, I followed him to a great fishing spot near Falls Creek Falls known as the "Toilet Bowl." The Toilet Bowl is a unique back eddy where a large amount of water pushes up against a huge boulder coming off the bank. In the backside of this back eddy is a calm, 20-foot piece of water that typically has hundreds of trout sitting in the soft pillowy water.

Surprisingly, the other guide passed up the Toilet Bowl. He just kept rowing right around the corner and set up to fish a different spot.

"Oh, this is gonna be fun," I chuckled. "Both of you, get ready to cast into the backside of the Toilet Bowl. You guys see that soft, flat, foamy water?"

They both nodded. As the boat stabilized, they each made a perfect cast, and their flies found the edge of the calm water. Instantly, two trout slurped their flies. They were both hooked up.

"Good work, guys!" I congratulated them. "Now we're gonna take these trout for a ride."

I rowed us around the corner with both of my clients' fish still on their lines. But this time, rather than staying behind him, I rowed right up next to his boat.

"Hey, man!" I said. "Are you from Idaho? I noticed you had an Idaho license plate. I'm from California. Some people say Californians can't fish. Man, I got really lucky with this double, huh? It's kinda blowing my mind, how I keep lucking into all these fish right behind you. Thank you for teaching me all the good spots on this river. You are one great guide. I really hope your clients feel like they're getting their money's worth. I think mine are!"

"F**k you, man," he said.

"What's wrong, man? I let you go ahead all day," I replied. "Just seems like you missed a lot of fish. I guess guides from California actually know some stuff. Good luck, Idaho–"

"You're gonna regret this," he threatened as he gave me the middle finger.

I smiled as I rowed away and finally netted my clients' two fish. We let them go, and my clients let out a massive laugh as we all basked in the joy of victory. The other guide had been humbled that day. Maybe even corrected. We all felt really good about it.

By the end of the day, with a clearer, calmer head, I regretted what I had done. I let my pride take over and became a big, angry, chest-pounding animal. I already knew I was a good guide; I already knew I had been on top of my game for awhile. All it took was another guide running his mouth to challenge that security. I felt myself wishing I could go back and confidently fish my normal routine instead of letting the other guide get under my skin.

In the end, I really got to learn my lesson. The next four times I used that boat launch, I returned to a slashed tire on my truck at the end of the day. Four times. I have no proof the other guide was responsible, but I can't think of another explanation. It makes a lot of sense: anger probably got the best of him too. A little mild, friendly competition is great for all of us, but every once in awhile, it goes too far, and our prideful egos call out our dark sides.

Ten years later, I still feel bad about what I did that day... but I still smile every time I think about it.

"THE FAVORITE 50"
CLIENT QUESTIONS

50. Does the river float in a circle?

49. Is fly fishing like playing Nintendo?

48. Do they have trout on Mars?

47. Can your drift boat go down Class 5 rapids?

46. Were you on the crew rowing team in college?

45. Why do all fly fishing guides look like racoons?

44. Can I use my spinning reel on your fly rod?

43. Is it cool if I spit my sunflower seed shells in your boat?

42. Have you ever taken an epic destination trip for bluegill?

41. What kind of bait do you use for fly fishing?

40. Can I dry-fly fish with an indicator?

39. Do you know of any fly fishing guides in Death Valley National Park?

38. Can I fish two fly rods at the same time?

37. Do you think Jesus Christ was a fly fisherman?

36. Do you know if dry fly floatant makes a good lubricant for sex?

35. What species of fish do you think would be classified as Jedis?

34. Would you rather catch a tarpon or a carp?

33. Why do you need an M.B.A. to be a fly fishing guide?

32. If I blindfolded you, do you think you could row us safely down the river?

31. Do the rocks make the river's current? *(Author's Note: Question asked of my guide friend, Brent)*

30. We have a trip scheduled two months from now. Can you tell me where and when to meet?

29. Ryan, have you ever rowed a drift boat before?

28. Is hiring guides similar to hiring high-end escorts?

27. Would you mind rowing with your shirt off?

26. Can you hold my beer while I reel this fish in?

25. Can trout turn into sharks?

24. Do you mind if I do a line of cocaine off the front of your boat?

23. Have you ever seen Quail Man?

22. Have you ever seen Bigfoot?

21. Can you teach me how to shadow cast like Brad Pitt from *A River Runs Through It?*

20. Is $5 a decent tip for our trip today?

19. Do you think that trout identify as trout?

18. What kind of pole do you like? *(Author's Note: It's called a rod!)*

17. Where have you been skiing lately to get a sunglass tan like that? *(Author's Note: Asked in the middle of summer.)*

16. If I don't catch a fish, do I get my money back?

15. Do you think brown trout are prejudiced against rainbow trout?

14. I don't really like fishing. Can I just get high and eat some snacks?

13. Can I use my two-weight fly rod for our steelhead trip?

12. Can I bring my Tenkara rod for our steelhead trip?

11. If I need to poop, do I just go in the drift boat?

10. Are fly fishing flies tied by tiny elves?

9. When are you going to get a real job?

8. Can you take this fly out of my ass?

7. Can you take this fly out of my crotch?

6. Is the river like Splash Mountain at Disneyland, where we ride a track back to the top?

5. Ducks can fly?

4. Ryan, have you ever fly fished before?

3. Ryan, have you ever fished this river before?

2. Do fish get more wet when it rains?

1. At what elevation do deer turn into elk? *(Author's Note: Question asked of my guide friend, Avery)*

THE BALLERINA

During my time on the South Fork of the Snake River in Idaho, I had the pleasure of guiding a professional ballerina from Paris. Colette and her boyfriend Pierre were on holiday, spending two weeks in the United States, including a stop in Jackson Hole to explore Yellowstone National Park and Grand Teton National Park.

Pierre already loved to fly fish for trout in Europe. A guided trip on the famous Snake River was an exciting piece of this visit for him. Colette had never fly fished before, but she was willing to give it a shot. Tall, beautiful, and graceful, most of her life had been devoted to ballet. After attending the Paris Opera Ballet School, she went on to make a career out of dancing. This would be the first professional ballerina in my boat.

We fished one of the lower sections of the South Fork, down

in the flatlands, surrounded by hayfields, grassy banks, and lots of grasshoppers. The constant clicking of the grasshoppers was music to our ears as we launched the boat.

Since Colette had never fished, I taught her how to cast, set the hook, and fight a fish. I gave her a quick lesson in dry-fly fishing. Then I handed her the rod, which she took with confidence, and immediately made a beautiful cast. Within two casts, she was exhibiting perfect form and rhythm, her line dancing back and forth.

In all my years of guiding, I've never seen anyone grasp the fly cast so quickly. It was as though all her athleticism, power, rhythm, and grace poured out from her arms into a casting masterpiece. Rarely am I in awe of casting, but a first-timer displaying such skill was completely mesmerizing.

I snapped myself out of my hypnosis to teach Collette how to set the hook and fight a fish. Again, she performed with precision. Colette was the most natural fly-caster I've ever had in my boat. I was so excited to share the joys of fly fishing with her.

With our quick lesson completed, we were on our way down the rushing river. The first grassy bank was just ahead, and I told Colette and Pierre to get ready for their first casts. They stood and pulled line off their reels.

Colette made a great first cast, her hopper landing inches from the grassy bank. Within seconds, a big, orange cutthroat slowly rose, opened its large, white mouth, and slurped in her fly.

"Set, Colette! Set the hook!" I yelled. "That's a fish! Set!"

To my dismay, she never lifted her rod. She only stared admiringly at the fish eating her fly. After the fish spit the fly, she looked down at me in astonishment and slapped me on the shoulder.

"Did you see that? That was so beautiful!" she said. "That trout came out of nowhere to eat the fly. I can't believe I just saw that. Let's do it again."

"Yes, that was awesome!" I replied. "We will definitely do that again. And next time, set the hook. When the fish closes its mouth on your fly."

Colette nodded her head in agreement and went into another cast. Moments later, Pierre hooked and landed his first trout of the day. Colette was so excited for Pierre; she took lots of photos to show her friends back home.

A few minutes later, Colette had her second chance at hooking a fish. Once again, a nice cutthroat lazily rose up to engulf her fly. Once again, she watched in awe and forgot to set the hook.

She smiled at seeing another fish and went into her next cast. Three casts later, a big-bodied brown trout exploded on her fly so hard, the water looked like someone had thrown a bowling ball off the top of the Eiffel Tower.

"Set, Colette!" I yelled. "Set! Set! That is a big fish!"

She stared into the water, enthralled by the sight of the fish taking her fly. She did not set.

After missing all three fish in the first mile of our drift, logically, I thought I should pull the boat off to the side and give Colette a chance to practice her hookset.

Beaching the boat on a gravel bar, I said to her, "Let's pretend to set the hook on a fish. Every time I yell 'Set!' I want you to quickly recast your rod. Recasting is the perfect way to set the hook."

Colette made a beautiful cast and her fly fell gracefully to the water. I yelled, "Set!" and she instantly raised her rod hand to her right ear to set the hook.

"Perfect!" I practically squealed. "That was perfect. Let's do it again."

Colette made another solid cast, I yelled, "Set!" and once again, she quickly "set" the hook. Colette had demonstrated she could properly set the hook. She passed the test. She was ready to go back to the grassy, overhanging banks.

I rowed to the second bank of the day. Instantly, Pierre landed another cutthroat. Then Colette got another grab.

"Set! Set, Colette! There it is!" I said.

Again, nothing. No body movement whatsoever. It was as though she was in the middle of a ballet routine, saw a fish, and forgot what her next dance move was supposed to be.

"Every time that fish eats your fly, you have to set the hook," I said. "Does that make sense to you?"

"Yes, I understand. I will try better next time," she said.

Colette went into another cast, and her perfect fly placement once again convinced another fish to eat her hopper. For the fifth time, she didn't set the hook. Could a language barrier be preventing her from understanding what I was trying to tell her? I decided to pull over a second time to show her how to set the hook again. But just like before, she was able to set the hook like a seasoned angler. So it seemed to me there was some kind of mental block preventing Colette from reacting to the fish in the moment. I was determined to figure it out.

I rowed downriver in search of more grassy banks. Suddenly Colette pointed in excitement to something out in front of the boat.

"Get the camera, Pierre!" she called out. "Water buffalo! There!"

I curiously looked in the direction she was pointing. I had never seen a water buffalo in Idaho before. I had seen lots of moose, deer, eagles, and a couple bears, but a water buffalo was a new one for me. As my eyes focused on the animals in the distance, I started to chuckle.

"What's so funny, Ryan?" Colette asked.

"Well, I hate to burst your bubble, but we don't have water buffalo in America. Those are cows," I said.

Pierre laughed out loud. Colette continued to peer downriver.

"Oh, wow. I have never seen black cows before," she said. "I just assumed they were water buffalo."

"Well, if you take a picture from here, I don't think your friends will be able to tell the difference," I told her. "You could tell them you discovered the first wild water buffalo ever found in the USA."

Colette giggled at the thought of trying to trick her friends. Pierre put the camera away, and we went back to fishing.

Colette stood up and began to beautifully cast her fly toward the bank. Once again she was rewarded for her great fly placement inches from the tall grass. Her hopper plopped onto the water and instantly a trout wanted to eat it. Then, like all the times before, she didn't set the hook.

For the next hour, fish after fish tried to eat Colette's fly, and never once did she raise her hand in an effort to hook one. None of what was happening made sense to me. She could do the practice hooksets effortlessly. Then, when she got onto the stage to perform, she would freeze. Pierre was hammering fish on hoppers, and Colette had yet to hook one.

I decided that Colette needed to fish from the front of the drift boat so I could watch better and try to understand her mental block. As we floated to another prime fishing zone, Pierre and Colette switched spots.

The boat was slowly drifting down the glassy river when Colette excitedly spoke up.

"Pierre, get your camera! Pierre, quickly! Look, ducks flying!"

Pierre dug through his backpack and grabbed the large Canon camera. Colette took the camera and snapped shot after shot of the mallards flying overhead. Satisfied with her capture, she turned toward Pierre and me with a huge smile on her face.

"Ryan! I never knew that ducks could fly!" she said. "My whole life, I have never seen a duck in flight."

"Really?" I replied.

"My whole life I have only seen ducks at the park near my house. They just swim around, quack, eat the bread we feed them…" she said.

"Yeah, we have that too. And in the wild, ducks fly," I said.

"That is so cool. I can't believe I just saw flying ducks. That was the highlight of my day," Colette gushed. Well, flying ducks or not, I still wanted to get her her first fish.

Pierre put the camera away, they grabbed their rods, and began casting. The fly fishing ballerina made her line dance through the sky and convinced yet another hungry and willing cutthroat to rise. Effortless finesse. As the fish inhaled the bug, I noticed Colette's whole body tense up. So she did react to the fish eating her fly, just not a hook set. I couldn't understand it.

"Colette, you seemed tense when the fish came for your fly. Are you scared of getting hooked?" I asked.

Colette shook her head no.

"What are you scared of?" I asked.

"I'm not scared of anything," she replied.

"Well, what was that?" I asked.

"I feel bad for the fish," Colette replied.

"What do you mean, you feel bad for the fish?" I asked.

"I don't want to hurt them. They are harmless animals and they don't deserve us tormenting them for fun. It's not like we are starving and needing to catch them for food. We are just doing this for the challenge and fun of it. Yet, these harmless animals are the victims of our efforts. I love seeing them and watching them try to feed, but I don't want to hurt them. So, every time they eat my fly, I cringe in hopes that they will not get hooked," Colette said.

"Oh my goodness. That makes so much sense now," I said. "You know how to set the hook, you just don't want to because it will hurt the fish!" Relieved to have solved the mystery, I went on trying to help her feel better. "Well, we're fishing barbless hooks...so the fish are being hurt minimally. Plus, we are practicing catch-and-release; we're letting them go."

"I understand all of that," she said. "I still don't want the fish to experience any pain."

Pierre jumped in at this point. "Honey, I think this may be the wrong hobby for you. The point of fishing is to catch fish. Not just to look at them."

Pierre made me laugh. And, I had an idea for him. For them both.

"You know, man...Colette's loving heart for animals doesn't necessarily mean that fly fishing isn't for her. I think there could be a way to do this to make everyone happy. Colette, let me see your fly."

Colette swung her fly over to me. I grabbed my pliers and cut the hook point off her grasshopper. Colette smiled and exhaled as the pliers clipped through the metal wire. *Liberte!* Freedom! Now she could cast to her heart's content with no worries of hurting innocent fish.

"Thank you, Ryan. This is going to be great. Today has been awesome," she said. "I am fly fishing with my boyfriend, I saw my first black cows, and I learned that ducks can fly. My friends at the ballet company will not believe all of this."

We spent the rest of the day admiring and celebrating fish as they rose to Collete's hookless hopper. Pierre, on the other hand, heartlessly continued to hook lots of trout, and landed them, too. Hopefully this difference between the two didn't become a source of conflict later in their relationship or, shall we say, challenge their longevity. It takes a special kind of woman to stand being married to a disgusting, heartless fly fisherman. I should know.

Go ahead and support conservation efforts, clip your barbs, keep 'em wet all you want...hooking fish is ruthless indeed.

YOU CAN DO IT!

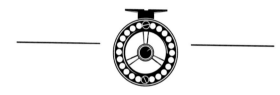

Being an angler is a journey down an extremely intriguing path full of twists and turns. The methods and destinations involved are seemingly endless. As soon as we think we have the sport mastered, there's a new technique to learn or a new species of fish to target. We will constantly be challenged throughout the journey. There is no singular mountaintop experience. Even the best anglers in the world are still on their endless journeys.

A lifetime of fly fishing adventures is akin to hiking the entire Himalayan Mountain Range, not just a single peak. Catching your first permit, or 20-pound steelhead, or 30-inch trout, or 50-pound striper is like summiting Everest. Any of those moments would be considered the pinnacle of one's fly fishing journey.

But what happens after the Everest moment? Do we just drop the mic and walk away? Do we climb back down the mountain and sell all our fly fishing equipment? Of course not! Experiencing that moment only enhances the desire to fish more. We get to the bottom of Everest, and we set the next goal of climbing K2.

The thing about the fly fishing journey is that somewhere along the way, we will encounter hardship, if our goal is truly experiencing all that fly fishing has to offer. Just like the climbers conquering the tallest peaks in the world, things get hard sometimes. Brutal weather conditions call out our mental toughness as we fish through the adversity. Sure, casting in 25-mile per hour wind is not ideal, but we can still give it a shot. We won't catch fish from the dock. As long as we've got a fly in the water, we've at least got a Lloyd Christmas chance of catching a fish.

When the river flow is high and many are tempted to stay back on land, it's an opportunity to push ourselves and learn something new. I'll let you in on a secret: *A lot of rivers fish really well when the flows are high.* Find the right spot, where the fast water slows down, and there may well be a higher density of fish in that area. Some of my most epic trips on the Lower Sac occurred when the river was at flood stage.

Days when the river was flowing 20,000 cfs, I would meet clients at the launch, incredulous we're still going fishing. The river may have been flooding, but the fishing was still great. We just adjust our methods and spots, thinking outside the box. If my clients are willing to do that, I tell them, I can guarantee it'll be a trip to remember. In fact, some of those flood events resulted in 100-fish days. Everywhere we found slow water, large groups of hungry and willing fish waited to be caught.

So we will be pushed to do things outside our comfort zones. We put on our big-boy underwear (or big-girl undies), take a deep breath, and rise to the challenge. Like when a climber encounters a storm on the mountain, there will be times in the fly fishing journey when our only option is to believe we can do it, and get it done.

Let me tell you about a client who was a great angler but didn't believe in herself. Cindy had the physical ability to climb Everest, but didn't believe she could do hard things. So when Cindy was confronted with difficult fishing situations, she would just give up.

In all my years of guiding, I'd never met someone quite like Cindy. She had an incredible cast and hookset. She was well versed in many fly fishing techniques. She was, in general, extremely confident on the water, catching a bunch of fish every time she went out. However, she lacked the confidence to land *big* fish. She had this false belief that she wasn't strong enough to land a fish of significant size. Every time she hooked a fish, she would say, "I hope this one isn't *big*."

If Cindy set the hook and believed it was a small- or medium-sized fish, she would do everything perfectly to land it. However, if she believed it was a big fish, she would instantly give up, pointing her rod directly at the fish to break it off–on purpose. For years, I watched Cindy hook and break off large fish. It drove me absolutely bonkers. I kept trying to convince her that she could land big fish, but she never believed me. She truly believed she didn't have the strength to land a large trout or steelhead.

One day, I was guiding Cindy on the Yuba River in Northern California. The Yuba is a medium-sized tailwater with some of the strongest fighting trout anywhere. The Yuba is not a top fishery in the West, but it's a great local trout stream for those who live nearby, with around 500 trout per mile, and a handful of steelhead mixed in to keep it interesting.

Cindy had landed a dozen rainbows in the 12- to 18-inch class, and every time she fought the fish perfectly. She set the hook firmly, kept her rod high, stripped quickly, and knew the exact amount of tension to apply to land each fish.

Everything was going well…until she tied into the largest steelhead I had *ever* had a client hook on the Yuba. As soon as she set the hook, the steelhead rocketed out of the water, showing every bit of its glorious 12 pounds. It took off faster than a dragster in the national finals.

"YOU CAN DO THIS, Cindy. Do not break off that fish!" I instantly yelled, acutely aware of her big fish fears. "That is the largest steelhead I've had hooked on this river – we are not letting that thing go. Keep that rod high, let the drag on the reel do the work. And believe in yourself."

"I can't do it, Ryan," she fussed. "This fish is too big for me."

"Cindy, I have clients with half your fishing skill who would try everything in their power to land that steelhead. Trust me, you can do this," I assured her. "Just play the fish like it's like a 16-inch trout. Pretend you didn't see it. Pretend it's small!"

"I'm not strong enough, Ryan," she said. "Did you see the size of that thing?"

"You are strong enough. Believe," I implored her. "Overcome the lie you're telling yourself. If you try to land this fish, what's the worst that can happen?"

Cindy looked back at me and nodded her head in agreement. "Okay, I'll try."

Just as those words left her mouth, the steelhead performed a multitude of cartwheels across the river, trying everything to free itself from the hook.

When Cindy eyed the fish the second time, her doubt took over. She pointed her rod tip at the fish and pulled back quickly to snap it off.

"NOOOO!" I yelled. "What are you doing?!"

As Cindy's fishing line recoiled back at her with no flies attached, a huge wave of disappointment came over me. I buried my face in my hands, knowing Cindy had purposely broken off the biggest fish I'd ever seen hooked on the Yuba.

"Cindy, when are you gonna learn you can handle more than you think?" I asked her. "You're a great angler. Your own lack of confidence is the only thing stopping you from landing the big ones. At least give yourself the chance to see if you can do it. Everyone loses big fish. That's partly how those fish get so big. But if you just give up every time, there's no way to know what you're capable of."

Cindy slowly sat down. "I just don't think I can do it. I'm sorry. One day maybe I will."

"It's okay. You're a great angler," I told her. "I just don't understand the mental block. Most people, me included, WANT the big fish. I've never had an angler break off a big fish on purpose."

Not all was lost. We fished our way through the rest of the afternoon. Cindy landed several more nice trout, and she was happy with her day. She had once again battled a bunch of regular-sized fish and had a ton of fun on her local trout river.

On the other hand, I was struggling. I was wishing any other client had hooked that big steelhead. Literally, any. It felt like a waste of a great fish, but who knows- maybe she'll grow from it. Sometimes growth takes time. I really wish she would have given it a solid try.

Fly fishing puts us in situations that challenge our comfort zone. Like Cindy, we'll question ourselves. Whether we can make a 40 foot cast into the 30 mph wind, avoid breaking the 6X tippet on a hookset, or land a 40-pound beast on a 10-pound leader. It'll help to believe we can do hard things. Or at least be willing to try and find out, and unafraid to fail. Never, ever point your rod tip at a large fish and purposely break it off. That shit is plain dumb!

BEGINNER'S LUCK

Friends, I am here to tell you that beginner's luck is a real thing.

In two decades of guiding, I have witnessed this supernatural force on numerous occasions. These chosen ones mess with our mental health by catching fish we have been hunting for years. While our fishing dreams teeter totter inside our fragile, fish-addled minds, our beginner friend shows up and catches fish from realms unknown to us. Is it luck or is it weird fish magic?

To fully appreciate the truly counterintuitive happenings I'm about to share, you must understand how powerful these moments are. I'm not talking about a buddy having a good first day and catching a handful of fish. Catching a trout on your first trip isn't a big deal. Heck, even catching a bonefish on your first try isn't that shocking. I'm not talking about a big chrome steelhead or a permit on your first day either.

I'm talking about the rarest of rare moments. Moments so fleeting that an entire lifetime spent attempting to recreate them would be in vain. Twice in twenty years my clients have caught true Lifetime Fish on their very first day of fly fishing. These are those stories.

One paranormal First Fish Activity took place on a spring day on the Lower Sacramento River near Redding, California. The Lower Sac, as most locals call it, is a big western tailwater flowing out of the Shasta Reservoir, and it's arguably one of California's best trout fisheries. The constant cold water coming out of the lake produces consistent bug hatches, which in turn, supports large rainbow trout, salmon, and steelhead. Having trout fished all over the West, the Lower Sac is as good as any other trout fishery I've been to.

The spring weather was beautiful and warm; the sun was out, the conditions were calm, and the whole universe was at peace. Larry, a long time client, brought his 11-year-old daughter Jennifer out for her first fly fishing trip.

Jennifer was such a cute kid. A 6th grader with a big smile, tons of energy, wearing lots of pink. Like her father, she was on the shorter side— maybe 4 feet 8 inches. Looking at her size, I wondered how she would handle the 9-foot, 6-inch, 6-weight fly rod I brought her for the day. Only time would tell.

To begin, I taught Jennifer the basics of nymphing, from the cast to setting the hook to what it feels like to fight a fish. After 30 minutes, she was getting a good handle on it; she seemed like a natural. Her cast was smooth and effortless, her hook set was quick and firm. She was a great listener, very enthusiastic to learn.

Jennifer was ready. We tried our first spot. It didn't take long for Jennifer to catch the first trout of her life—a beautiful 19-inch rainbow. Unlike most first fish, she didn't panic and was able to do everything right. She set the hook, made two quick strips to get good tension on the fish, then let the line slide through her stripping fingers when the fish ran toward the middle of the river. She wore out the feisty rainbow in short order. We netted the trout, took a couple grip-and-grin photos, and released the fish to fight another day.

Little did we know that Jennifer and her beginner's luck were about to enter into interdimensional worlds I had not yet fished.

I rowed down a bit to fish a well known spot. It's a slow, deep current line in the middle of the river. For the patience it takes to watch an indicator sloooowly float down the seam, there's usually a couple rainbow rewards each day. It's not the most enjoyable or exciting spot, more like fishing a slow-moving pond, but it's very consistent. For a young beginner like Jennifer, I was happy to give her something easy and reliable.

She casted her flies out into the slow-moving foam line and intently watched the indicator move down the current line for a couple minutes. Suddenly, the indicator went down hard. Jennifer, with her 11 year old whack-a-mole reaction time, set the hook quick and firm. She came tight to the fish, and the fight was on.

Two hard head shakes had the rod throbbing back and forth. The fish made a deep run and the line jumped off the deck, running through Jennifer's fingers. Like a seasoned fly fisher, she slipped the line to the reel, then listened to the reel sing as the fish pulled out the entire fly line.

The fish got about 100 feet from the boat, then stopped and sat on the bottom. There were no more big runs, no aerial displays. Just pure stubbornness. With all her might, Jennifer gripped that rod and cranked the reel to gain line back as the fish allowed. And in rebuttal, every 20 seconds or so, the fish would take a few feet back, just to let her know he wasn't giving in.

Ten minutes of Jennifer pulling hard on this fish got me wondering – had she hooked a king salmon? Trout rarely fight longer than a couple minutes. The fish stayed on the bottom of the river, giving her a couple hard head shakes to remind her who was boss.

I kept encouraging Jennifer to stay with it. Despite her small stature, she had great resilience and strength tugging back on her mysterious fish of the depths. Another five minutes went by before the fish gave to rising in the water column.

Jennifer kept her rod high and reeled in the slack. I kept telling her to keep hard pressure on the fish. After 15 minutes, it seemed like she had finally worn that fish out. And here it came, heading to the surface.

My heart stopped at first glimpse of the fish. Jennifer had hooked the biggest rainbow I had ever seen on the Lower Sac!

As the fish slowly came up to greet us, I readied my net. First chance I got, I quickly scooped up the slab. Jennifer's second fish, ever. The massive rainbow measured 28 inches long and had more girth than Cartman from *South Park*. Jennifer had just landed a legitimate nine pound rainbow trout.

All three of us let out a celebratory roar. Larry, veteran angler that he was, gasped, "HOLY SHIT. Holy shit! That is the biggest f***ing trout I have ever seen!"

Jennifer looked back at her father, suddenly looking a whole lot more like her mother. "Dad! We don't cuss like that," she admonished. "You told me to never say those words. Those are bad words."

"I know, honey, but that trout is f***ing enormous," Larry said. "I've been fishing for 30 years and never caught anything close to that big. That fish is a f***ing monster!"

"Dad, watch your mouth," Jennifer insisted. "Mom wouldn't like you saying that."

"I'm sorry, honey. I know that cussing is bad, but holy shit, that is a fish of a lifetime," Larry said. "You could fish the rest of your life and never catch another trout that size."

I sat there enjoying the banter. Their father-daughter dynamic was hilarious. In 20 years—thousands of days guiding the Lower Sac—the client who caught the biggest rainbow was an 11-year-old girl, on her first day of fly fishing, dressed head to toe in pink.

Was it pure beginner's luck? Or did the fish gods send down a blessing that would leave me envious of this tiny person standing in front of me? I've been fly fishing since I was her age; now, in my 40's, I'm still trying to find the fish Jennifer caught on her first day.

Ten years after my trip with Jennifer and Larry, another client's catch would make an even stronger argument for the fly fishing paranormal. Bill had hired me to take him striper fishing on the Sacramento River near Chico, California. We were fishing the same river where Jennifer learned from her father how to properly cuss, but about 125 river miles south, where the river water is warmer.

This would be Bill's first attempt at catching a species other than trout; he was hoping to expand his fly fishing repertoire. Unfortunately, Bill didn't realize how difficult it is to cast a shooting-head fly line, or that all his years of casting floating lines for trout would be of no use to him in the learning process.

Before fishing, I gave Bill a casting lesson, teaching him the basics of a shooting head. After about 10 minutes of instruction, I handed Bill the rod to try it out. As expected, the first few casts were poor and ugly. Bill could barely cast 20 feet. Realistically, he would need 40 to 50 feet to have a chance at Sac River stripers. There's a better chance of Yoda switching to the Dark Side than an angler catching a striper with a 20-foot cast in the Sac. I encouraged him to keep trying.

Like several casts before, Bill's next few casts also went 20 feet. I took the rod again and gave him some tips to cast more line. To my dismay, and Bill's, none of his next several casts exceeded 20 feet either. Bill's casting lesson took more than an hour, over which time he showed no improvement.

At this point, Bill was getting frustrated, and I had run out of casting tips. It was the first time I was unable to teach someone the basics of casting. I was at a loss for what to do next. So I told Bill he would be baptized by fire, learning as we fished. I hoped he would pick up the technique throughout the day, gradually improving with practice.

At the first run, I got the boat into position and told Bill to get ready. Bill stood up and promptly made a 20-foot cast.

"All right, Bill. Nice try. Go ahead and strip up the line and try again," I said.

Bill quickly stripped in the slack dangling below the boat and casted a second time. Just like the cast before, it went about 20 feet. The third cast was the same. The fourth cast too.

Bill's face fell, dejected, presumably questioning why he couldn't cast farther than a kindergartner can throw a ball. The effort was there, but no progress.

His line still dangling in the water, Bill persevered. He began to strip his line in to make his next cast.

"Um, Ryan? I think I got one?" he said.

I snapped my head around to see Bill's rod bent, the tip bouncing back and forth.

"YEAH, you got one!" I exclaimed. "Strip hard. Keep stripping 'til it feels like that fish is gonna rip the rod outta your hand."

Bill stripped two more times before the rod loaded deep into the butt section. The fish slipped the 20 feet of slack off the deck and the line connected to the reel. The reel sang as the fish went for a huge run upriver, taking 150 yards of Bill's backing with it.

"I think you got a good one!"

Bill nodded his head in agreement. His shooting head cast had a ways to go, but he knew how to fight a fish. He kept good, hard pressure the entire time. After about 10 minutes, the fish began to tire and we got our first look at the surprise customer from the Dangle Diner—an enormous white and silver striped bass.

Bill made the last few cranks on the reel, then directed the fish toward my hands. I gripped the striper's mouth with two hands and hoisted the 30-pound monster over the gunwale.

"Let's go! Let's go!" Bill hollered. "Look at that fish! That thing is a monster!"

We took a whole bunch of hero photos, and after the fish was revived, I let go of her tail and watched her slowly swim back to the depths of the Sacramento River.

I sat down in my chair mesmerized, eyes on the floor, reflecting on what all had just transpired, shaking my head in disbelief.

"Ryan, you seem really taken aback," said Bill. "Aren't you excited?"

I looked up from the floor of the boat.

"Yes, totally excited for you," I said. "That was an insane catch. The striper you just caught is a fish of 50 people's lifetimes. There's no way to explain how or why you caught that fish. Your fly was literally dangling below the boat. There was no reason for that fish to eat a dead-drifting fly with no movement. Stripers don't behave that way. I'm trying to make sense of this, and I can't."

"Well, don't be a Debby Downer, man," Bill said.

"I don't think you get it," I replied. "I have clients who've been fishing for stripers for 40 years and have never sniffed a chance at a striper that size. I have clients who would literally donate one of their kidneys to be in your spot right now. For that to be the first striper you ever caught, on a non-cast, with no movement on your fly, it just doesn't add up. I really don't get it. That is so far past beginner's luck. I've fished this river more than 100 times, never hooked a fish close to the 30-pounder you just got. Trust me, I am excited for you. But, damn, I am jealous and confused."

Every summer, Facebook reminds me of Bill's monster striper, and every time, I still shake my head in disbelief. I think I'm still a little jealous. He had no perspective on what happened that day. He literally lucked into a fish the rest of us yearn to catch. Why did he get to catch that fish? Who knows? Maybe it was beginner's luck. Maybe it was a twisted, paranormal present from the fish gods to mess with my psyche. I do know this: some fish just don't add up.

Good luck to all you beginners out there. May the fish gods have mercy on you and your terrible casts.

PIERCINGS

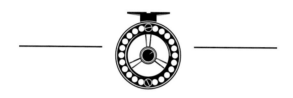

Fly fishing, for the most part, is a pretty safe sport.

Yes, there is risk involved in any outdoor pursuit, but compared to other fresh-air activities, fly fishing tends to be on the tamer side. Hunting, skiing, surfing, and even rollerblading are all more dangerous than fly fishing. Probably the most dangerous aspect of our sport is being surrounded by water. A boat could sink, we could fall and have our waders fill with water, or we could lose our footing and be swept into a swift current.

Removing those extreme and rare events from the equation, maybe the most dangerous aspect of fly fishing is the sharp hook zipping back and forth through the air as we cast. Getting hit by a fly mid-cast is a lot like being shot with a pellet gun. It doesn't feel good. It's a damn good reason to always wear sunglasses when you're fishing. No one wants a fly in their eyeball. The odds are low, but stick around long enough and you'll hear about it.

It was a dark, rainy day on the Lower Sacramento River in northern California. I was guiding two guys. The fishing was excellent; we were catching lots of big rainbows. With all the rain and the dark, cloudy conditions, one of the guys removed his sunglasses. Logical.

Within minutes, he and his buddy got their lines tangled on their back casts. The guy still in glasses cast forward, and the line came taut. Instantly, the guy without glasses fell to his knees. His hands shot to his face as he cried, "My eye! My eye!"

One of my greatest fly fishing fears had finally come to pass. I reached out, put my hand on his shoulder to steady him, and said quietly, "Take a deep breath. Try to get calm. When you're ready, turn around so I can look at it."

He took a few seconds. Slowly he turned around, his face now uncovered. I slowed my breathing to center myself, readying for my patient, having reached legitimate terror levels just by my own imagination. A closer look revealed the exact location of the fly.

It was caught on the edge of his upper eyelid. The barb, still visible, had not penetrated his skin. The sharp hook point was mere millimeters from his eyeball. This was actually the good news. I breathed a huge sigh of relief.

"You're okay," I told him. "The fly is *not* in your eyeball. I'm gonna reach up and gently take the fly out of your eyelid. It's just your eyelid."

I gingerly pinched the fly between my thumb and forefinger. Then I gently pulled down on it. At first, the eyelid pulled down too, but the fly popped out easily enough.

My client, now crying tears of relief, gave me a hug.

"God was watching out for you today," I told him. "That was really close. I'm so happy you dodged that bullet. Before our next trip, get a pair of yellow lenses so you have protection for rainy days."

In fact, every angler should own sunglasses with yellow lenses. In the middle of a massive storm with super-dark, low-light conditions, yellow lenses will not only protect your eyes from hooks; they will also make it look like you're fishing in the sunlight. Better fishing and keep your eyeballs.

In addition to that eyelid, I have removed flies from a cheek, an earlobe, a throat, a mustache, a butt, a leg, and countless hands. Hooks are sharp, designed to penetrate a fish's bony mouth, so they easily pierce human skin. Luckily, there's a fishing line trick that easily removes a fish hook from skin. If you don't know it yet, look it up on YouTube before your next fishing adventure. This trick will save you lots of pain, and possibly a visit to the emergency room.

Of all the hooks I've ever removed, one in particular was especially precarious. It was a normal spring day on the river. The sun was shining, the sky was bright blue, the birds were chirping in the crisp morning air. My clients and I were floating down a smaller river in my drift boat, approaching our next fishing spot, when we happened upon a man and his dog on the edge of the river. The man was panning for gold. His dog was happily pacing up and down the bank, splashing in the water.

The riffle I wanted to fish was directly across from them. It was far enough away that I didn't think we would bother them.

"Okay, guys. Get ready to fish the next drop-off," I told my clients. "You wanna cast into that shallow riffle, then allow your fly to fall off into the deeper water. Whatever you do, don't cast until we're past the gold panner. Don't hook the dog on your back cast."

They nodded in agreement and stood up, each making two false casts to get their line out. Then, on the third false cast, I heard the dog yelp loudly. I looked over my shoulder to see the dog running up and down the bank like it had just been bitten by a rattlesnake…except my client's fly line was trailing behind it.

"Holy shit, dude," I said to the offender. "You just hooked that dog! You gotta be kidding me. How did you do that?"

"Oh, my God. I can't believe I just did that," he said.

I quickly rowed over to the bank to help the dog. Surprisingly, the gold panner was so locked into finding his next treasure, he didn't notice all the commotion. I got the boat to the bank and dropped my anchor. The dog was now completely still, seemingly in shock at what had just happened to him.

I slowly stepped out of my boat and walked over to the dog. My eyes scanned the dog for the end of the line. As I got closer, I realized the dog had been hooked in the most unlikely spot. There, on the tip of the dog's penis, was my client's red, size-16 Copper John nymph.

You're going to think I'm making this up. It doesn't seem possible. I know. But it really happened.

I didn't know exactly what to do yet. First, I cut my client's line to remove any resistance from the dog's sensitive nether region. This is when the gold panner finally noticed me squatting next to his dog.

"Everything okay?" he asked, standing up.

"Not really," I said. "I'm sorry to say, my client hooked your dog."

"Oh, that's okay," the gold panner responded. "He's a tough ol' dog. Bet it won't phase him one bit."

"Well, this one might," I told him.

"What do you mean?" he asked.

"Well, my client somehow hooked your dog in its...penis."

"What the hell?"

"Yeah, I have no idea how the fly got there and hooked him where it did," I said. "The good news is, we're fishing barbless, so the fly should come out easily."

The gold panner walked over and finally spotted the red fly.

"Holy shit," he said grimacing. "Now that's something you don't see very often. Do you wanna get it out or should I?"

I sincerely appreciated the offer. "Since it's your dog, I think it's best if you do it," I said.

We coaxed the dog down on its side, and I slowly pet him as the gold panner reached down with his leathered hands, timidly pinching the fly between thumb and forefinger. The dog immediately yelped and its head shot off the ground. We helped him calm back down as his master slowly pulled the hook out.

"I'm sure glad you guys were fishing barbless," the man said. "You want your fly back?"

"No, I think you should keep that one," I told him.

"Thanks, man," said the gold panner, standing up. "I'll add this to my collection. I've never seen this fly before– is it a good one?"

"Sir, that fly is so good, it catches all kinds of things," I told him. "From trout to penises, it has you covered."

MAN'S BEST FRIEND

Nothing compares to enjoying the outdoors in the company of your dog. Whether you're out for a walk or a hike, hunting birds, or fishing, having a dog by your side makes the time more fulfilling. "Man's best friend" makes a lot of sense out there.

Felines may be superior hunters, but I don't recall ever hearing about someone bringing their cat on a hunting or fishing trip. That said, there must be someone in this world who's taught their cat to retrieve a mallard—and if that someone is you, I would love to hear about it.

Dogs were created by God to do things cats can't do—chase balls, hunt pheasants, retrieve dead ducks, and provide unwavering loyalty. I guarantee you, no human in your family is as loyal as your furry friend. As long as you feed your dog, show it kindness, maybe play with it here and there, it will do almost anything for you. Does that mean your dog won't get into trouble and give you some gray hairs from time to time? Absolutely not. When our dogs run away, chase the UPS truck, harass the neighborhood squirrels, or roll in a pile of cow dung, we can't help but shake our heads in frustration. Or maybe pull out some hair.

There really is something deeply satisfying about seeing your animal out in the wild, running around, sniffing animal trails, tapping into its true nature. I love to see our Great Pyrenees running around our property with a big ol' smile, tongue dangling out of her mouth. She seems so free when she's out there roaming, inspecting, protecting her people. Definitely one of her happy places, and ours too.

Dogs and hunting have gone hand-in-hand for thousands of years. Many species have been bred to help man hunt animals: foxes, racoons, bears, mountain lions, and all kinds of birds. But when was the last time you heard about an incredibly talented fishing dog? Fishing dogs are not normal.

Over the years I've had lots of clients bring their dogs on fishing trips. Some were perfect boatmates, but many would've been better off left at home. Some folks have such a great connection with their dog, taking them everywhere, they don't consider the tight confines of a drift boat when they hire a guide to take them fishing. I guess they see it as another fun activity for their dog to participate in.

With three people in a drift boat, an animal in the mix is not ideal. Boat space is limited to begin with, and adding a dog makes it extremely tight. Any time a client asks to bring along their furry friend, it always gives me pause. On two occasions, clients brought their small dogs in the boat, and both times I accidentally stepped on their dogs while netting fish. It's hard enough keeping my balance netting a fish in a boat that's bouncing and weaving through the river's currents without worrying about a lapdog underfoot.

On a different occasion, my clients brought their black lab on the boat. In general, labs are great fishing dogs. Bred for the water, they love to be outside, and usually have a warm and pleasant demeanor. However, this lab couldn't find a comfortable spot to sit. My clients didn't want the dog sitting by them for fear of their lines getting tangled in the dog's feet.

With no other space to be, the lab decided to sit between my legs. That was fine when I had to row, row, row the boat gently down the stream. But when I had to dig into the water and stroke hard on the blades, I smacked the dog in the head with my oar. The lab let out a small yelp, which prompted its owners to turn around and glare at me.

"Sorry!" I gritted my teeth. "My oar handle got him. We really need the dog to sit by one of you so I have more space to control the boat."

"We don't want him near us," one of them said. "We don't wanna risk losing a fish because he got tangled in the line."

"Well, if he's not with you, he may get hit a few more times today," I said. "Are you okay with that?"

"It's a dog," the owner said. "He has a strong head. Try your best, do what you need to do."

For the rest of the day, that damn dog sat between my legs as happy as a clam. About once an hour, he'd get a small bonk on the head from the oar as I tried to navigate the river. It was an awkward position to be in; I knew they cared about their dog, but they also didn't want him interfering with their fishing trip. I really didn't like hurting the dog. I wondered if his nice day out on the river was worth all those bonks. Wish I could've asked him.

On another trip, my client Jake brought his lab, but he didn't mind the dog sitting up next to him. Throughout the day, the fly line would get wrapped around the dog's feet, and I would hop up to assist with the tangle. It was no big deal, though; Jake and his dog were just happy to be out on the river together.

Around midday, we were fishing down a fast-flowing, boulder-strewn bank. Jake cast his large dry fly up toward a soft, foamy current line behind a big rock, and a huge mouth engulfed his fly. He set the hook firmly. We both saw a 25-inch brown thrash its body back and forth with three massive head pumps.

"That's a big one!" I yelled loudly. "Let it run!"

As soon as those words left my mouth, the fish jetted out toward the heavy current of the river. Jake began to slip his line when, suddenly, it came tight around his dog's feet. He reached down to clear the line, and in all the excitement, *he tossed his dog out of the boat!*

The lab whined for his owner as he tried to navigate the fast and turbulent current. Within seconds, he was floating away from us. Somehow, with all this going on, Jake was able to clear the line and was still connected to the incredible brown trout.

"Shit, Jake, your dog is struggling," I said. "We gotta go get him. Break that fish off."

"Don't worry about him," he said. "Help me land this fish! I never hooked a trout this big in my life!"

"I think your dog is more important here," I replied. "There's always more fish. We could seriously lose your dog."

My words seemed to resonate with him. He turned his

head to see his dog's entire body go under the water. No more yelping, just a dog fighting for his life.

"Screw your fish, man, I'm gonna go save your dog," I said.

I rowed hard with every muscle in my body to speed up the boat. The dog was 100 feet away. As I closed the distance, the animal went through a series of small rapids. That lab was doing everything it could to keep his head out of the water.

Jake still hadn't broken off the fish. I rowed hard downstream with his rod pointed upriver, about 75 feet of line hanging in the water. My rowing was increasing the distance between the boat and the brown trout, but I was getting closer to the dog. I still had to navigate the turbulent water we were floating through.

"All right, I need your help here!" I yelled at Jake. "I can't get off the oars, it's too dangerous. Grab your dog, pull him in!"

"Can't do that, Ryan," he said. "I'm fighting a monster trout at the moment! You get the dog."

"Get your shit together!" I yelled louder. "Have some perspective. What's more important: the dog or the fish?"

"This is what you're paid for, Ryan," he said. "We can do both. You get the dog, I'll fight the fish."

The boat went over another low-rolling wave. As it crested the next one, the dog popped up two feet from us. I quickly let go of the oars, grabbed the lab by its coat, and threw it into the boat hard enough that he bounced off his owner's leg.

"Ouch, man," he said to me. "That hurt. Be careful."

"Dude, I'm trying here," I told him. "I can't row the boat, keep us safe, save your dog, and watch your fish all at the same time. That's why I asked for your help."

The dog did two massive body shakes, splashing water all

over us. As soon as he got situated, I shifted my attention back to the fish. Jake's line was stretched out behind the boat, and somewhere 100 feet behind us was a massive brown trout.

Within seconds, his line tightened and ripped off his reel.

"Ryan, this fish is really running!" he said. "Look at my reel spinning. I can't turn the fish!"

"You're stuck on a log," I said.

"No, I can still feel the fish pulling hard," he defended.

"Trout don't pull that much line," I said. "After all that went down with your dog in the water, you're gonna lose this fish. Just point your rod at it and break it off."

He thought about it, nodded, and reluctantly pointed his rod at the fish.

"It's not breaking," he said. "Look, my reel is still spinning. What do I do?"

"Hold the handle of the reel; don't let it spin anymore," I told him.

Jake grabbed the handle. The line stretched and finally broke. It was, in fact, stuck on a log, and he lost his entire fly line. It was an expensive mistake, but nowhere close to losing his dog.

"Wow, what a wild ride..." Jake remarked as he slowly reeled in his backing. "That felt like something out of the movies."

I shook my head in disbelief and finally pulled over to the side of the river to get a different rod strung up for him.

Not the best dog-gone-fishin' memory. I hate to say it, but most of my guiding days with dogs haven't been that great. That said, I do remember some incredible moments. My absolute favorite dog in the boat was a short-haired springer named Sage who had been fly fishing on the river his whole life. (And, yes, he was named after the rod maker.)

Friendly and warm-hearted, Sage loved people and loved being on the boat. He sat in the front of the drift boat next to his owner Toby. Sage had a special knack for watching intently as the indicator floated down the river while we nymphed along. When Toby casted, the dog's head went back and forth, following every false cast. With the indicator settled in its new spot, Sage locked onto it with eagle eyes, and every time the indicator went under the water, the dog barked loudly. Usually, I'm the one yelling at my clients to "Set! Set! Set!" But these days, all we needed was the dog. Sage was literally an indicator alarm, going off every time his master had a bite.

The funny thing was, Sage was only really amused by trout measuring about 20 inches or more. If Toby hooked an average 16-incher, Sage just quietly observed the action. But when Toby fought a big one, Sage would jump up and down in excitement. Apparently, Sage had learned from Toby that we only get excited for larger trout. And when we did land a 20-plus-incher, Toby held the trout in front of Sage's face, Sage looked at it for a sec, then Sage gave that fish a big, sloppy lick. Once Sage got his lick, Toby set the trout back in the water to be released.

In all my years, I've never met a fishing dog as cool as Sage. He was like a new kind of superhero, come to Earth to save distracted fishermen struggling with staring at an indicator all day long. Who knows, maybe I need to train my dog to do that. It would make my job a whole lot easier. I would never have to yell "Set!" again.

If you're thinking about inviting your dog on your fishing trip, make sure he or she is ready for it. And don't assume that just because you hired a guide for the day, he'll be cool with you bringing your 150-pound Saint Bernard along. Sometimes there's space, sometimes there isn't. Respect your guide; after all, we want you to have the best fishing possible. Most of us are dog lovers, but that doesn't guarantee we're down with having your dog up in our business all day.

And keep in mind, your furry family member will always be more important than any fish you hook. Trust me, your kids and spouse won't forgive you when you try to explain to them, "I couldn't save Lassie because I was trying to land a fish of a lifetime."

Rest in peace, Lassie. But no resting in peace for you, my friend.

BABYSITTING

Watching kids catch fish is just pure delight. It doesn't even have to be your own kids. The joy expressed by any kid hooked up to a fish...it's electric.

Just *thinking* of my own kids catching a bluegill, bass, or trout warms my heart. I'm blessed to have two girls who want to fly fish with their dad. They do enjoy fishing, but I know they enjoy the quality time with Dad even more. Getting away from our normal routine, being out on the water, connecting with the outdoors and each other, it's truly refreshing. I hope they always want to fish with me, even into old age. I dream of taking them all over the place, chasing fish and hanging out with them. I know as they get older, their interests will change, and their time will be consumed by friends, sports, and boys. Still, I will always hope to take them fishing.

Good thing they do grow up. Because let's be honest, fishing with kids is a blast, but it also has its challenges. I've been fortunate to teach hundreds of kids to fish over the last two decades, learning a few tricks along the way to keep them in the game. Depending on your kids' ages, there are things you can do to keep them entertained and fishing longer. For example, only fishing the best spots increases the chance of catching more fish, having more fun, and, ultimately, wanting to fish again and for longer periods of time.

One of my goals is to preserve their desire to go fishing. I want them to want to fish again! So they need to have a good time. As parents, if we set our own fishing ambitions to the side temporarily, we can support our kids in simply discovering the joy of fishing.

One summer, guiding in Idaho, two of my clients had a very different idea about what was best for their young sons. These two dads had brought their boys to a high-end lodge in Idaho to fish the world-famous South Fork of the Snake River for their very first fly fishing experience. How cool is that? Well, at least, that's what I thought. Usually when fathers bring their sons on a fishing trip, the dads fish with their kids. However, these two dads had a different idea.

When my guide buddy and I met our clients at the fly shop, it was the first morning of our 4 days together. Our clients informed us they had each brought their own son, and I would be guiding the kids, Cody and Jackson, all four days. These fathers had assured their wives that this was a special father-son fishing trip, but actually it was just an excuse for the two men to fish. With some very expensive babysitting.

Cody was a whopping 6 years old, and Jackson was 8. A

word of advice: When determining whether your kids are old enough for the hands-on joy of fly fishing, I've found at least 10 years old is generally your best bet. Any younger is a lot more challenging. In my experience, 6 and 8 is too young for handling even the basics. Share the joy of fly fishing another way instead – stories, videos, photos, hang out by the river and watch, visit an aquarium, take a boat ride. Share your enthusiasm in ways they can handle. I was sitting squarely behind the 8 ball with these tykes.

We hopped into our trucks and started down the road toward the boat launch. A typical driving-to-the-river fly fishing conversation was not on the docket that morning, replaced instead with talk of Paw Patrol, Legos, and the latest Disney movie. Instead of answering questions like, "What kind of fish will we catch today?" I got, "What's your favorite *Monsters, Inc.* character?" and "Do you like Legos? What's your favorite—Ninjago or City?" I laughed as the boys peppered me with questions driving along the beautiful Snake River.

We got to the boat launch and readied the boats and rods for the day. As I put the rods together, the boys ran around like cowboys and Indians cracked out on Mountain Dew, wreaking havoc on the morning's peaceful sunrise. Meanwhile, their dads were off to the side, laughing with the other guide and drinking their first beers of the day. They were completely checked out now that their boys were in the care of their fly fishing babysitter.

Since I'd have them in my boat all four days, I wanted to make sure I spent enough time teaching them how to cast dry flies, set the hook, and fight the fish properly. I handed Cody the fly rod first and began to teach him how to cast. Just 6 years old, he could barely hold the rod with one hand. I quickly determined he needed to learn the two-handed cast. You're probably thinking, "You don't cast dry-fly rods with two hands." Well, you might be right, but I didn't know what else to do. The kid should have been fishing a Snoopy rod, but all I had was a nine-foot 5 weight.

Not surprisingly, his casting was pretty terrible. Cody didn't have the strength to hold the rod. With all his might, he could barely get it to move forward and back. His flies would slowly flop here and there as he waved the rod in the air. It was like watching a 98-year-old Dick Van Dyke learning how to fly fish for the first time. Cody could get his dry flies about 10 feet from the boat—not a great distance, but I knew I could help him catch a fish if I could get in the right spot.

Jackson had a couple years on Cody, and it showed. With enough muscle mass to handle the rod, and about 30 minutes of coaching, Jackson was getting the basic concepts down and landing his fly about 20 feet from the boat. At that distance, you can catch a ton of fish on the South Fork, so I expected he would have an easier time than Cody.

Once the boys grew comfortable with casting, setting the hook, and fighting a pretend fish, we pulled up the anchor to head out on our fly fishing adventure. These kids would need easier spots where their limited casting skills had more potential, and the first such spot was about a mile downriver. As I gently rowed, Cody spoke up.

"I'm hungry. Do you have anything to eat?"

"Yeah, sure, buddy," I said, reaching over to my cooler. "The lodge makes us a great lunch. Let's see, you've got a bag of chips, a cookie, a turkey sandwich, potato salad, and an apple."

"What kinda cookie?" Cody asked.

"Looks like…white chocolate macadamia nut," I replied.

"Yeah, I don't like those kinda cookies," he said. "What kinda chips?"

"Ummm, looks like Nacho Cheese Doritos," I told him.

"Yeah, I don't like those kinda chips," he said. "I guess I just won't eat. It's okay."

"How about half a sandwich? Or an apple?" I asked. "If you're hungry, it'd be good to get some food in your belly so you have energy for catching those big fish."

"I only like salami. I don't eat turkey. I *really* don't like apples. I only eat grapes and strawberries. The only chips I eat are the blue ones—vinegar. And I only like chocolate chip cookies."

Oh boy. "Cody, did your dad pack you any food in your backpack?" I asked.

"No, he said you had my lunch."

Any parent or person who hangs out with children knows I was absolutely screwed. If you are the parent of a picky eater, sending them out on a big all-day adventure, you pack them their own food. Rather than helping Cody have a great introduction to fly fishing, his dad left him high and dry with nothing he would eat. Maybe Dad hoped Cody would expand his food tastes, but a drift boat with a stranger for a long day on the mighty Snake River seems like a funny place to try that. Needless to say, I was feeling nervous about what the day had in store for us. Hungry turns to hangry with very little warning, and food is the only cure.

We arrived at our first easy fishing spot of the day. I had the two boys stand up and get ready for their first casts.

"Okay, boys," I said. "Look downstream there at that big

boulder. Now see behind it, do you see that soft, foamy water behind it?"

Both spun around and looked upstream.

"Boys, downstream is the other way– turn around," I said. "Hey, let's use your rod as a pointer so you know where to fish. Now, point your rod to the left."

They both pointed their rods to the right. Right, my bad.

"Oops, hang on, left is the other way. Now see that big rock coming up? See that flat, foamy water behind it? I want you to cast your flies into that foamy water."

They pointed their rods at the target. "Good!" I said. "Right there!"

Just as they were about to start casting, Cody spoke up. "I'm bored," he said. "I don't wanna fish anymore."

"Okay, buddy. I hear you," I said. "Just try for another couple minutes. I wanna get you a fish! But you gotta cast! Get ready to cast in 10 seconds."

The boat drifted past the large boulder. "Okay, go!" I called out. Cody hooked his shirt, and Jackson forgot most of what he had just learned. He waved his rod back and forth, tangling faster than Jimmie Johnson at a NASCAR race.

I pulled the boat to the side of the river. First, I got Cody's fly out of his shirt. Then I addressed the bird's nest of Jackson's fly line, leader, tippet, and flies. Ten minutes later, everyone was fixed up, and we headed back out into the strong current of the river.

Now rowing to the second easy spot of the day, I heard Jackson speak up. "I need to go to the bathroom."

"Why didn't you go when we were stopped on the bank?" I asked.

"I didn't have to go then. I need to go really bad now," he replied, squirming in his seat.

"Gotcha. Do you need to go number 1 or number 2?" I asked.

"What's that mean?" he asked tentatively.

I giggled at his innocence. "Do you have to pee or poop?"

"Pee! I would never poop in the woods! Who would do that? There are animals out there! They would see me pooping. I only poop in private," Jackson replied.

"I totally get it," I said. "But sometimes you just gotta go and try not to think about it. You know what? One time I had to poop in front of a deer."

"No way! That's disgusting!" Cody said loudly.

I smiled as I rowed to the riverbank to let Jackson out of the boat.

"Okay, Jackson, no worries. I'll make sure to find you a private spot where no animals will be peeking," I told him.

"Thank you," he said. "I don't want any animals seeing my..."

"Yep, gotcha–" I replied.

When we got to the riverbank, I dropped my anchor and pulled us up to a safe spot.

"Okay, Jackson. I'm looking all over and I don't see any animals," I said. "It looks safe for you to get out and pee."

Jackson climbed out of the boat and walked toward the bushes. Most anglers would have stopped after the first bush, but Jackson really wanted privacy. He kept walking, passing bush after bush, into the deep, dark, towering cottonwood trees, completely out of sight.

"Jackson! Don't wander too far!" I yelled.

After a few minutes, he came back into view with a little pep in his step. He was smiling ear to ear as he approached the boat. "That was a good spot. No animals saw anything. Thank you."

So we continued our journey down the river. At this point, we had been on the water for more than an hour, without one legitimate cast. I decided to row for another mile to get to one of the best spots in the river—an eddy where hundreds of fish lived.

As we got close, I told the boys to stand up and get ready to cast. I slid the boat into the big, foamy eddy and saw lots of trout just below the surface, surfing the current line. The boys casted. Cody's landed in the water this time, about eight feet from the boat. Jackson's landed about 15 feet out.

Cody's flies were too close to the boat to catch anything, so I focused on Jackson's as they bounced along the bubbling current line. Suddenly, a nice cutthroat came up and slurped in his big foam stonefly. Just like we practiced, Jackson quickly threw his rod back to set the hook.

"I got one! I got one!" Jackson yelled. "What now?!"

"Reel, buddy!" I said with excitement. "Use the reel like we practiced."

Jackson proceeded to reel backwards.

"Not that way; reel the other direction," I told him as his fly line tangled inside his reel. I quickly reached up and pulled out the slack.

Jackson made the quick adjustment, reeling the correct way. He kept his rod tip high and took his time wearing out the cutty. I grabbed the net and Jackson directed the trout toward me. With a smooth scoop, we landed Jackson's first-ever fish. He immediately jumped up and down in a happy dance.

"I got one! I got one! I caught a fish!" he screamed.

With the fish still in the net, I leaned over to give Jackson a high five.

"Yeah, you did! Way to go, Jackson! You did it!" I celebrated. "Let's get a picture of your catch to show your dad."

"Do I have to hold it?" he asked. "I don't wanna touch it. It looks gross."

"You don't have to hold it if you don't want to," I told him. "I can hold it, and Cody can take our picture."

"Okay, good. Yeah, that fish looks slimy. You hold it for me," Jackson replied.

I set up the camera and handed it off to Cody, crossing my fingers. Then I softly grabbed the fish out of the net, and posed with Jackson to capture the incredible moment. Jackson was smiling bigger than a clown at a birthday party full of kids. He was so proud of his catch.

Cody snapped the picture, we released the trout back into the water and redirected our attention to the fishing. We fished the same spot for the next 10 minutes but couldn't get the flies in the right spot to fool another trout. So I rowed downriver half a mile and came to another good spot.

The boys stood to cast, and once again Cody's cast fell short while Jackson's led to another beautiful cutthroat trout. He was just as excited about catching the second one as he was the first. I was pumped for him. He was really starting to get the basics down. A few more celebratory pictures with a slimy fish, and we started fishing again. However, Cody was feeling frustrated.

"I don't like fishing. I'm not good at it," he said. "Fishing is stupid. I hate this. I wanna go home."

Small tears formed in Cody's eyes. Slowly, the first tear ran down his cheek.

"Oh, buddy, it's okay to feel frustrated. Even the grownups get frustrated sometimes. You've never fished before! You can't be a pro on your first day. Just keep trying, and you'll catch something."

"You promise? I'll catch something?" Cody asked.

"Yes, I promise," I said.

It felt like a big risk to make a promise like that, but I knew I had some spots downriver where Cody's chances would be really high.

I turned around to Jackson and said, "Since you've already caught two fish, and Cody hasn't caught any, I'm gonna let you take a break and give Cody a turn by himself, see if we can get him one. You've been doing great! So take a seat, reel in your line, and just enjoy the ride."

Jackson agreed it was a good idea to get Cody on a fish. As we floated along, Jackson just looked around and took in the scenery of the Snake River.

Eventually we arrived at a beautiful, shallow gravel riffle, where the water was flowing at the perfect speed with a great green drop-off right in the middle. As we got into position, I told the boys, "Keep your eyes on where the water changes from brown to green. If you watch there long enough, you'll see a few fish rising."

"I see one!" Cody exclaimed.

"I saw it too!" cried out Jackson.

"There's another one! Another! Lots of fish!" Cody said excitedly.

"Yep. These fish are here every day," I told them. "Plus, we're here at the perfect time for the hatch. Cody, I think you have a really strong chance of catching your first fish right here. Cast as far as you can and try to get your fly to land a couple feet in front of the fish."

"Okay, I'll try," Cody replied.

His two small hands worked hard to cast the rod back and forth. He finally got them working in unison and made one final hard cast forward. His flies went about 12 feet.

"Good start! Now do it again, Cody. If you can go about five more feet, we'll have a solid chance," I said.

Cody used all his might in his little arms, picked up his cast and sent another one out there. The line slapped the water hard, but his leader stretched out and his fly landed right where it was supposed to. Surprisingly, a fish came up and aggressively attacked the fly.

"Set! Set! Set, Cody!" I yelled in excitement.

Cody leaned back and swung on the rod as hard as he could. The rod came tight; he was hooked up to the first fish of his life. The trout felt the sting of the sharp hook and rocketed toward the middle of the river. Sadly, Cody wasn't ready to let the fly line slip through his fingers, and the fish broke off.

Cody's whole body went limp. His head dropped to his chest, his arms held the rod motionless, and the brief, chilling quiet was broken by the sound of a heartbroken child crying. Cody turned to us with tears rolling down his cheeks, then sat down and stared at the floor of the boat. In an instant, Cody's sadness flashed to anger.

"I told you I wasn't good at this!" he said, glaring at me. "Fishing is dumb. I never want to do this again for the rest of my life. You promised I would catch a fish. You're a liar!"

"Cody, I am so sorry you lost that fish," I said. "But! I'm excited you made a good cast, and you set the hook really well!

Before this, you didn't do any of those things. Do you think when Babe Ruth swung his first baseball bat, he hit home runs? Or do you think he fouled off a bunch of pitches before he sent the ball over the fence?"

Cody didn't answer. He just kept staring at the ground.

"Cody, what do you think Babe Ruth did, when he was just starting out playing baseball?" I asked again.

"He probably messed up a bunch," he grumbled.

"Exactly. When we're learning something new, it takes a bunch of tries before we hit the home run," I told him. "That fish you just lost, that's like fouling off a pitch. But the batter gets back up there and swings at more pitches. He doesn't give up! Eventually he gets a home run! But he's gotta swing at a lot of pitches! As a fisherman you gotta do the same thing. You gotta get back up there and make another cast, and another one, and another one. Do you think you can try again?"

Cody slowly nodded his head in agreement. "Yeah, I can try…"

I peered back into the riffle. Cody's hard cast and short interaction with the fish had put down the whole pod of rising trout.

"I think we should go downriver to a special spot where I catch a fish every day. This entire season, there's always been a fish there," I told Cody. "You can have this spot all to yourself. Before we do that though, I think we should try to eat something to keep our energy up."

I grabbed our lunches out of the cooler and passed them around. Jackson and I instantly dove in to our turkey sandwiches. Cody opened his lunch and poked around.

"I told you, I don't like any of these things. I'm not hungry," Cody said sharply.

"You seem like you're hungry. I think you should try to eat something," I told him. "How about this? I'll give you a dollar if you eat one chip."

"Really? A dollar? But I already told you I don't like those chips," Cody replied incredulously.

"Yep, I'll give you a dollar. Have you ever tried Doritos?" I asked.

"No. They look gross," he said.

"I think they're delicious." I reached into my boat bag, pulled out my wallet, found a dollar bill and laid it on Cody's lap. "All right, bud. If you eat one whole chip, that dollar is yours," I said.

Cody looked pretty enticed by the dollar. He opened the Doritos and stared into the bag. He gave it a sniff and grimaced. Eventually he pulled out a single chip and inspected it. With his eyes closed, he put it in his mouth and began to chew. *Crunch, crunch, crunch.*

Cody looked down at the bag again, eyebrows raised. "Huh, not so bad."

He grabbed a second chip and ate it. Then a third and fourth. Before long, he had devoured the whole bag.

"Thanks for the dollar!" he said with an orangey, crumbly smile.

"If you want to make another two dollars, you can eat that whole cookie," I said.

"No, thank you. I don't like those cookies," Cody replied.

"Have you tried white chocolate macadamia cookies before? They're great!" I told him.

"No, but they look gross. I don't want any, thank you," Cody said.

I just nodded my head in agreement, not wanting to push

him any further. He had just taken a step in overcoming his food fear, and my goal of getting something in his stomach was accomplished. Jackson and I finished our lunches, so it was time to give Cody another shot at catching his first fish.

I rowed the boat down to a log jam that had been really good to me all season. Getting the boat into position, I peered into the dark water to see if my fish friends wanted to come out and play. I told Cody to cast up next to the log. It was only 12 feet away, so I knew he could make the cast. The fly landed perfectly right next to the log, and a big 22-inch cutthroat came up to inspect his fly. It tracked the offering for a few feet before slowly retreating to the log jam.

Internally, I was yelling at the fish. "EAT THE FLY! Throw me a bone here!"

"Cody, make another cast up there," I said. "Let's see if that fish will come up again."

The fly landed nice and soft. The fish popped out of the log jam again to inspect it. As with the previous cast, there was something about the fly the cutthroat didn't like.

"Cody, make another cast," I said. "That fish is interested, we just have to convince it your fly is real."

Cody's third cast was awkward and ugly. He put too much power into a cast that only had to go 12 feet, and the fly slapped the water harder than a 400 pound man in a belly flop contest. To my surprise, the large cutthroat shot up and engulfed the fly.

Cody set the hook perfectly. The battle was on.

This time he remembered to let the line slip through his fingers and engage the drag on the reel. With all the strength his arms and shoulders could muster, Cody held the rod up high and fought the fish well. The big cutthroat started rolling wildly under the water, as cutts often do, and tangled itself in his leader. With the fish motionless in the water, Cody pulled the rod hard to the right to let me scoop up his catch.

The three of us let out a celebratory scream all at once. The boys jumped up and down, and I had to join them. Cody beamed with joy. I unwrapped the beautiful golden cutthroat from Cody's leader.

"Can we take a picture to show my dad?" Cody asked.

"Of course," I said. "Do you wanna hold it or should I?"

Cody held out his two small hands with a big grin on his face. I placed the cutthroat in his hands and he held the slimy fish like a seasoned angler. We took a few pictures and released the cutthroat back into the cold water. The fish swam right back to his home under the log jam. After we watched the fish swim away, there were high fives all around.

"Cody, that was so awesome. I think you need a nickname. How about *Babe Ruth*?" I said.

"Why?" he asked.

"Because you just hit your first home run out of the ballpark!" I replied.

Cody smiled. "I like that nickname."

We spent the rest of the afternoon trying to catch a few more fish, but none were in the cards. Babe Ruth ended up with his one big cutthroat and Jackson got his two. The boys were happy with their first day of fishing. No doubt, it was a rollercoaster of emotions as they learned a new sport, but considering their ages, they hung in there really well.

In fact, Cody's cutthroat turned out to be the biggest fish of the group that first day. His dad was so proud of him, not to mention amazed at the beautiful cutthroat Cody had landed.

On the boys' second day of fishing, they progressed a little more. Babe Ruth landed two and Jackson caught four. The third day, four and seven. Then, on the last day, they each landed more than a dozen trout, both catching more fish than their fathers.

By the end of their trip, I think they realized fishing was just as cool as Legos, Paw Patrol, and video games.

I'm still astonished the dads fished by themselves for four straight days and never spent any time on the water with their sons. Their sons discovered something new and special, but it seemed to me the dads missed their chance. I got to make some young friends who would prepare me to fish with my own kids later in life. I trust my daughters will hit one out of the park one day too, catching the biggest fish. But no babysitters; I'll be there to see it.

CELLULAR

Over the last 10 to 15 years, cellular phones and smart devices have rapidly become a fixed part of our everyday lives. The cell phone is an amazing piece of technology, making many aspects of our lives simpler and more efficient, though in some ways, more complicated, too. No longer do we have to wait for the paperboy or the news anchor to find out what happened in the world yesterday. No longer do we have to watch the 6am news to figure out that the meteorologist has a 50/50 chance of predicting the weather correctly. Our cell phones now do these things for us, and more, 24/7.

No longer can we impress our friends at the bar with random sports trivia. Maybe you still got it, but inevitably someone will pull out their phone and Google how many touchdowns Joe Montana threw in his career. When it comes to facts, the truth machine is now at our beck and call.

Smart phones have made fly fishing both easier and more complicated. It's so much easier now to keep track of river flows, current weather patterns, and tides. We can look at our weather apps and get an hourly forecast any minute of the day. Weather apps have saved countless days on the water. Instead of the morning news' "storm on the way today," our app tells us what time this storm could start. And we can keep coming back to it, using that info to make fishing decisions and safety decisions.

No longer do we wait for the newspaper to read outdated fishing reports. Now we scan blogs, websites, and social media to piece together the exact fishing information we need, increasing our chances of success on the next fishing trip. YouTube gives us access to free videos about casting, rigging fly rods, tying knots, and presenting our flies. I remember, back in the day, I had to walk into a fly shop to buy a VHS tape to learn all that. With so much fishing knowledge available on the internet, nobody has an excuse for not knowing how to tie a blood knot.

The smart phone camera is also a source of newfound simplicity. We no longer need to pack a camera (and film, and batteries) in order to capture photos of our catches. No more lying to your friend at the bar about the 35-inch brown trout you caught on your local river. Proof is easily obtained now, and expected; pull that phone out and scroll to it if you want to be believed. And when your friend sees the photo of the not-quite-35-inch brown, be prepared for that friend to call bullshit. Maybe somewhere between your third and fourth beer, you inflated a 29-inch brown trout grew by 6 inches.

The cell phone camera is a complicated subject. On one hand, it makes life and fishing easier because it's readily available, but the social media frenzy drives those who partake to feel they need a photo or video of everything. I've got a frequent client who insists on a selfie with every fish. He doesn't want me to take a nice photo of him holding the fish he just caught. He wants a selfie: a crooked, awkward picture with his big mug and a part of the fish. Every fish— not just the big fish, but literally every fish he catches. I know social media has elevated the selfie, but I just gotta say, his photos are terrible. Imagine Mr. Selfie picking up his every-single-fish prints at his local drug store back in the day.

For all the ways our cell phones make our lives easier, they also make our lives much more complicated. In a lot of places I guide, cell signal is available the entire time. Great for an emergency, but I really think it's a shame my clients no longer have the opportunity to take a break from regular life during their days on the water. Many of us go fishing to escape work demands and family obligations, or to just give our minds a rest. It's harder now to immerse ourselves in the environment, the calming water, and the challenge of the chase. Try losing yourself in the great outdoors when your wife is calling to ask where the car keys are, every damn work email is another ding, and everything has a false sense of urgency. The self-control required to resist peeking at your cell phone is…fleeting.

For the best day on the water, may I suggest an unwritten rule: Turn It Off. You are spending time, money, and energy to go fish, so be there. This applies to both anglers and guides. My friend and I had a guided trip for redfish down in Texas, and the guide's phone literally rang all day long. Every 15 minutes or so, his Nickelback ringtone, "Look at this photograph, Every time I do, it makes me laugh…" would play loud and clear. The worst part? He answered every call. We listened to this guide talk on his phone for half our trip as he poled us around the South Texas flats. We came to take in the beauty of the flats and chase redfish tails, not to hear about his plans to meet up with his friends at the bar that evening.

It's common for my clients to scroll through social media every time we move fishing spots. No longer do they look around, admiring the unique beauty of their surroundings. Now they're more entertained and interested by what's in that mini-computer. Which is strange because the latest posts on social media will still be there when they get home, but the bald eagle flying overhead will not.

Some clients insist on uploading photos to social media while still on the water. I understand wanting to celebrate our latest catch with loved ones; I don't understand skipping out on fishing time. In this crazy modern world, "instant" is every-thing. Catching a fish isn't enough; blasting that photo out as soon as possible for "likes" and "comments" makes it complete. What happened to the simple joy of the accomplishment?

One winter day, I took a phone call from an executive assis-tant. He called to book a spring guide trip for his boss, Eddie. I had never fished with Eddie before; his assistant found me on Google. I chatted with the assistant for a few minutes and learned that Eddie was a top executive for Verizon Wireless. After talking through options and details, we decided Eddie would fish the Feather River for the spring steelhead run.

A few months later, Eddie's day had come. It was an early meet up, so I was at the boat launch getting the boat ready in the dark. A few minutes after our arranged meeting time, a black limousine pulled up to the launch area. I was taken aback–I had never seen a limo in a boat parking lot before. The chauffeur smoothly exited the driver's seat and walked around to open the rear door. A middle-aged man stepped out of the limo with a bag and a fly rod case. Was this my client for the day?

Sure enough, the man walked over and greeted me. "Hi! Are you my guide for the day?"

"Yes, sir, I'm Ryan," I told him, offering my hand for a shake.

"Okay, good. My name is Eddie. I'm glad to make your acquaintance. I'm really looking forward to steelhead fishing today. There's nothing better than catching steelhead," he replied.

I nodded, still trying to process the limo. He was dressed like a typical fly fishing client: a nice Patagonia shirt, jeans, athletic shoes. What really caught my eye was his belt. More specifically, the four cell phones attached to it. It called to mind the belt of a law enforcement officer: a pistol, handcuffs, pepper spray, billy club, maybe a taser, all posted to their assigned position. Well, Eddie's weapon of choice was…cell phones. Lots of cell phones.

"Eddie, that's alotta phones you have there," I said.

"Yeah, it's pretty ridiculous. Sadly, it's part of my job," he explained. "So many different people need to get a hold of me. I have multiple phones with unique rings for different reasons. It helps me track which calls I need to answer and which calls I can ignore. Anyway, I'm excited we're starting early this morning; I get to fish a whole hour before business hours."

"You mean you're gonna get calls on all of those phones today?" I asked.

"Yes, I need to take business calls as we fish today. Will that be a problem?" Eddie replied.

"No, not at all. You're paying me to take you fishing," I said.

"You do whatever you need to do on the water. We can literally just float down the river and not fish if that's what you need."

We got everything ready for the day and pushed out into the river. Eddie was an accomplished fly fisherman, and it didn't take him long to hook and land his first steelhead of the day. Thirty minutes later, he landed his second. As the sun rose, so did Eddie's smile. He was having a great morning.

Around 8:30am, one of his cell phones rang. He peered down at his utility belt. "Sorry, Ryan, I have to answer this one," he said. "Can you pull over and give me a few minutes?"

"No problem," I said, rowing over to the bank.

We sat for about 10 minutes while Eddie took his business call. When he finished, I rowed back to the top of the run, and Eddie made another cast. As his flies hit the water, a second phone rang. Eddie quickly looked down at his belt. "Damn, I have to take this one too," he said.

"No problem, I got you," I said, again rowing to the bank.

This phone call was a bit more heated than the first. Evidently there were problems at Verizon's headquarters that morning. As I tried not to listen to Eddie's conversation for the next thirty minutes, I wondered how many more calls he would get.

With that phone call finished, Eddie turned back to me. "I'm sorry, Ryan. We have a bunch of problems at the office this morning. My staff is calling for input on how to handle them."

"It's totally okay. We all have responsibilities, I get it," I replied.

This run really deserved another chance, so I rowed back to the top, got the boat in position, and Eddie made another cast into the riffle. We were mid-drift downriver when a third phone rang. Eddie unclipped the phone and answered it, his flies still drifting downriver. He handed me his rod as if I had a spare hand. I tucked the oars under my knees to reel in his line.

This time, I didn't row to the side of the river. "Go with the flow," I thought, to our next fishing spot. When we reached it about 10 minutes later, Eddie was still on the phone. I pulled over to the bank. To fill the awkward space, I grabbed my phone to catch up on the latest social media posts, including yesterday's client and his selfie dump from the day before. I laughed at his awkward photos, trying to be cool with his little rainbow trout.

Eddie wrapped up his phone call 20 minutes later. "Enough of that!" he said. "Let's get to the reason I'm here. You ready to fish again, Ryan?"

"I think the question is, are you ready to fish again?" I laughed.

"Absolutely," he responded.

Eddie finally got 30 minutes of peace. He caught his third steelhead of the day. After landing the beautiful, bright chrome spring steelhead, he gave me a big high five.

"Ahh, I love this!" he said, glowing.

Just as the happy words left his mouth, another phone rang. Now it was a personalized ringtone, a song. Eddie dug around in his bag, pulling out a *fifth* phone, and answered it. This call was his wife with a quick question about his plans for the day.

As soon as Eddie hung up, I couldn't help myself. "That has to be some kind of record, Eddie!" I said. "You have five phones on you!"

"Yeah, it is pretty sad, huh?" he said. "I wish I wasn't so tied down all the time."

"Why do you have all those phones on when you're trying to relax and get away from it all?" I just had to ask.

"Who said I was trying to get away from it all?" Eddie asked.

"Well, I just assumed…aren't you trying to have a peaceful day on the river?" I responded.

Eddie laughed a big belly laugh. "No, not at all," he said. "Most of these people think I'm in the office right now! The way I see it, I caught three steelhead this morning while working. How cool is that? Here I am, in the middle of the river, catching these awesome fish, and they think I'm at the office! Aren't cell phones amazing?"

Honestly, I was surprised, but suddenly it all made a lot more sense.

"Wow! Okay, that is not what I thought you were gonna say, but I totally get it now," I said. "Most of my clients hate it when their cell phones ring out here. But you're technically at work."

Eddie nodded and grinned. "Let's go find another steelhead."

"You bet." I rowed downriver to our next fishing spot when Eddie's belt blew up. All four phones began ringing at the same time. He looked down in confusion. "What the hell? Why are they all ringing at the same time?"

Methodically, like a surgical nurse setting up the OR, he pulled all four phones out of their clips and lined them up side by side on the tray in front of his seat. He contemplated which one to answer first, his hand hovering over each one. Finally, he made his pick and let the other three go to voicemail. I would have loved to hear his process of elimination.

Eddie jumped into a very heated conversation with a fellow executive. Something major had happened; they needed Eddie, not just working, but actually in the office. This phone call continued for several more minutes. Every thirty seconds or so, a different phone would ring again on the tray. He kept hitting the ignore buttons, trying to focus on the situation at hand.

When that phone call was finished, he answered the next. Then another one. For the next hour, Eddie played whack-a-mole, answering as many questions as possible for his co-workers.

Finally, the phones stopped ringing. "I'm sorry about that, Ryan," he said. "There's a major ordeal at work today, and there are a lot of fires to put out. I hate to say this, but I need to get off the water and into the office as soon as possible."

"Okay, I'll start rowing to the takeout," I said. "Just a heads up, we've got about 10 miles left in our drift. It'll probably take me 2 hours to get you off the water. I'll row hard, but we have a long way to go."

"Ummm, yeah, I don't have that kind of time," Eddie replied.

"Sorry, man. Drift boat problems. I wish we were in my jet boat, I could just hammer down the throttle and get you back in a flash," I said. "But I have to row the next 10 miles."

"Yeah, I get it. Let me see what I can do," Eddie said.

Eddie grabbed a phone. This was the first time all morning Eddie was the one initiating a call. He spoke to his assistant, creating a plan to get him back to the office as soon as possible.

"Okay, I think I have a plan that will save me a bunch of time," he said. "My assistant has ordered a helicopter to pick me up from the river. It will be here in 20 minutes. Can you find a big gravel bar where the helicopter can land to pick me up?"

"Did you say a *helicopter* is gonna pick you up from the river?" I asked. "I've never seen that before!"

"Yeah, I've done this a couple other times when big things

happen at work," Eddie responded. "It's no big deal. Just find a big, open space where the helicopter can land safely."

"Okay, you got it," I replied, a nice open spot occurring to me. I started my row downriver.

Just five minutes later, I pulled up to the large gravel bar and dropped anchor. I helped Eddie get out of the boat and put his fly rod away. He grabbed his bag and packed up all his phones.

Within minutes, we heard the heavy blades of a helicopter flying the river in search of Eddie. As the helicopter flew over us, the pilot waved to acknowledge us and then made a U-turn. Next thing I knew, he was landing the helicopter 200 feet away on the open gravel bar.

"Well, that's my ride," Eddie said. "Sorry I had to cut our day short. I had an absolute blast landing three awesome steelhead this morning. I like tipping my guides well, so here's $500 for putting up with all this bullshit and putting me on some fish. I hope to fish with you again one day."

I smiled and shook Eddie's hand, wishing him good luck with the rest of his day. He trotted to the helicopter, climbed in, and off they went. Several minutes later, the thunk-thunk-thunk of the helicopter was gone, and peace had returned to my boat.

As I quietly rowed down the river, I felt intrigued. What must have happened to warrant an emergency helicopter? It must have been really important to interrupt an excellent morning of steelhead fishing. I was bummed for Eddie, his fishing cut short, but with his optimistic, flexible mindset and financial status, I figured he would have plenty more opportunities to get his fishing fix.

Thirty years ago, Eddie would have just "gone fishin." Whatever happened in the office that day would've waited until the next morning. He would have fished in peace and enjoyed all that the river has to offer.

I wonder if cell phones are really *good* for us. Yes, they are great for so many things, but are they good, for *us*? I'm not convinced. There are downfalls to being connected to everybody, everything, everywhere, all the time. Cell phones are a blessing when you really need that advice, or that helicopter, but they are also an absolute nuisance, and as much as they connect us, they disconnect us from what is truly important–being where we are. Presence, peace, the people in front of us, a clear mind, they're all lost thanks to the convenience of the cell phone.

When I'm fishing, my phone is silenced in my bag. Consider it. Get back to the root of why you're truly out there on the water. Don't worry, you can let your guide take the pictures, and you can still post them– when you get home.

REEL RELATIONSHIPS

Most of the friends I've made in my adult years are people I fish with. A common bond between two people is a great chance for a friendship. In my early years, I thought guiding was about entertaining people and helping them catch fish. As I've matured (though I'm not sure I've completely gotten there yet), I've realized that fishing is an opportunity to create deep, meaningful relationships with my clients.

Something special happens when you fish with someone year after year. The more fishing we do with a person, the more we get to know them. The conversations grow from just fishing to other, deeper topics like family, religion, current events, and real life. What started as a fishing relationship slowly turns into a friendship.

And a friendship forged on the water has a different, special element to it, a natural, raw, stripped down feeling. The natural environment is grounding, calming, enabling people to relax and let their guards down. The water brings peace, which creates presence, and availability. This leads to connection. Maybe what's happening is, when we're out on the water, all the distractions and busy-ness and our coping mechanisms and defenses aren't pulling us in a hundred different directions. It's all stripped away, and we can be fully present to ourselves, to what we're doing, to who we're with– making us way more available for forging a friendship. Plus, it's several hours, which is rare quality time these days.

In Northern California, there is no off-season. NorCal fly fishing guides fish year-round for a variety of species, including trout, steelhead, bass, and stripers. In the winter we chase chrome-bright, ocean-fresh steelhead in the redwoods. Spring brings large hatches of aquatic insects, creating some of the best trout fishing anywhere in the country. The summer months offer warm, sweaty days casting topwater flies with explosive strikes from largemouth bass. Summer also includes running jet boats on the rivers in search of monster stripers lurking in the structure. This year-round bounty means lots of repeat clients, with greater frequency.

Some find this hard to believe, but in my California days, a handful of clients fished with me more than 30 days a year. Fish with a person 2 or 3 times a month, for 10 years, and you can become very close friends. Over time, I got to know quite a bit about them, from their families and their beliefs to their childhoods and their struggles. They also got to know a good deal about me. It's a beautiful and vulnerable space, not one we enter into with just anybody. But fly fishing can be this vehicle, for the right people, this soul space.

No longer were our days focused solely on catching as many fish as possible. Lunch breaks sometimes lasted twice as long. Inside jokes flowed freely. No more urgency to get to the best spots, to outfish other guides on the river. Days on the water got shorter, as the friend time seemed to satisfy more than a few more fish ever could. Goodbyes in the parking lot lasted longer. Now dinner was included in the trip because we weren't quite done yet, even though next week was already booked.

These longtime, repeat clients now feel more like my extended, and chosen, family members. They're the people I call for advice, when I need some insight into life. Some of them call me for the same reason. One of my dearest friend-clients calls me his "river therapy." And it's good for me too. I have been blessed beyond measure to have found such incredible people to fish with.

Many of my guide friends can attest to this friendship-building power of fishing. Here is one of their inspiring stories.

Jason and Mike's friendship had actually begun before Mike was born, as Jason was friends with Mike's family first. As Mike grew up, he showed a strong interest in fly fishing. Jason, years ahead of Mike and an avid fly fisherman, took Mike under his wing, teaching him all the basics.

Jason owned a very successful business, and chose to enjoy his wealth - and his life, and his favorite people - by taking his friends and family on guided fly fishing trips. As Mike got into high school, Jason took him on guided trips too, and over time, Mike's passion for fly fishing only grew. His instinctual ability to catch trout and steelhead was obvious. After high school, Mike held a variety of jobs to make ends meet, but nothing was as satisfying as being on the water. Mike decided to dive into guiding. In his eyes, nothing could be better than getting paid to be on the water.

Of course, Jason would be Mike's first client and biggest fan. Jason hired Mike to take him on adventures all over. The student had finally become the teacher. And Jason loved every minute of it. In time, student/teacher transformed into a deeper bond: true friendship. These two souls had an understanding, a respect and a deep love for one another.

Jason's business continued to flourish, providing the ability to fly fish the world. And he couldn't imagine doing it without his buddy Mike. Jason and Mike traveled the world together, and Jason was happy to pay Mike's way for whatever new adventure was in store for them. Their bond continued to grow.

Jason would become Mike's top client, hiring Mike every other week for the entire year. Sure, Jason appreciated hooking fish and drinking beers, but what he really loved was being on the water with his buddy. For years, the two of them chased fish together. Mike had it good, and he knew he was blessed to have Jason as a friend and client.

Eventually, Mike found a wonderful wife—beautiful, outdoorsy, warm, strong, and supportive. He had found his soulmate, the best catch of his life. They were perfect for each other. It wouldn't take long for the two love birds to expand their nest with a couple beautiful babies, two boys a few years apart, who also loved the outdoors and their family. This family found great connection as they explored the natural world together.

Jason became a beloved uncle to Mike's boys. Birthday parties, family holidays, special gatherings...Jason loved being part of the family, and loved supporting Mike as a father and husband. If one of the boys had a baseball game on the afternoon of a scheduled trip, Jason made sure Mike made that game. Jason may have loved to fish, but he knew there was more to life than fishing. He didn't want a busy guiding schedule to keep Mike away from what was truly important.

Just when life was about as perfect as possible, life kicked Mike in the balls. His wonderful wife was diagnosed with cancer. It took several years of chemo and radiation treatments to overcome the disease. Through many, many hard days, much determination, and a deep desire to be there for her boys, she was able to beat the cancer. Throughout the illness, Mike stood by his wife's side, supporting her every possible way. "In sickness and in health" was a promise he had meant.

Cancer gave Mike's family a new perspective on life. Life is too short to wait to enjoy it. Mike and his wife decided they wanted to make their dream house—a home where they could raise their two young boys and put roots down deep into their community. A home where they could bless their friends.

For two years, Mike spent every free hour working on their dream home. He hired contractors for the big projects, but at night, after guiding, he spent countless hours putting his own blood, sweat, and tears into the property. Slowly but surely the house came together. Half of the home was built by Mike's own hands, and the other half was paid for by guide trips. Lots of guide trips.

When their dream home was finished, they had a huge celebration. Life was good. His family was healthy, he had built their dream home, and he was chasing his dream as a fly fishing guide.

The family settled into their new chapter, content as could

be. Then, more disaster found its way into Mike's life. Six months after finishing their dream home, a terrible forest fire hit his community. The flames ripped through Mike's property and destroyed their home. Mike was crushed.

It wasn't about losing money; their home was insured. Mike had poured himself into this home for his family; he had given two years of this short, precious life, only to have their home destroyed. What was once a beautiful lot of pine trees and native bushes now looked like a burnt moonscape of dirt and rocks. A force of nature had stolen so much joy and life.

Being a man of courage, Mike took his time to reflect and find his purpose again. He didn't give up. He knew he had to show his boys how a strong man reacts to tragedy. He got back on his feet. He absorbed life's massive punch. This man would not let life keep him down.

They started rebuilding their home again. This time, Mike let the contractors build the house. He didn't have any more to give. Who could blame him? A year later, the replacement home was built, and they were finally able to move back in.

Life returned to "normal." The kids were in school and playing sports. Mike was on the water building his guiding business, and his wife was healthy. Life was headed back in a positive direction. He was becoming quite the guide legend. Mike was happy. He had withstood his wife's cancer and losing a home. He knew he was a stronger and deeper man for going through those tragedies.

Then, more hardship found its way into Mike's life. His wife's cancer returned. Mike was crushed. This time the cancer was more aggressive and had spread through more of her body, and she needed special treatments. The doctors suggested treatment from Stanford University Medical Center, more than four hours away from their hometown.

This time, Mike was struggling to hold it together. The last five years had been horrendous for his family. Mike had been strong through it all, but this time was different. This punch was so big, he didn't know what to do next. He hoped his wife could overcome the cancer again, but how could he be with her and still provide for his family? Mike had to figure out how to support his wife, help his boys find their way through, and pay all the bills. It seemed like too large of a mountain to climb.

Then one day, he got a call from his fishing buddy, Jason. Jason knew Mike was struggling. After a few minutes of catching up, Jason told Mike, "I just put one million dollars into a trust account with only your name on it."

"What do you mean?" said Mike, stunned by the words. "Why would you do that?"

"Mike, I love you, buddy. I know life has been brutal for you the last few years. I also know you can't afford to absorb another blow like this. I know your wife needs these treatments. God has blessed me in lots of ways. You need help, and this is one way I can help. As your family goes through this next battle, you need the flexibility to take days off to care for your family. You need to spend time together. You've gotta be the stable force in the family, and that means you can't be gone guiding all the time. So pay for medical bills, go get the treatments, be with your wife, take family vacations together, do everything you can to be present. It pains me knowing the hard times you have been forced to endure. I am so grateful that my friend and fly fishing guide has become like a son to me. I love you, Mike."

Mike didn't know what to say. Tears welled up. Tears of

confusion and tears of joy. Tears of sadness, for all the pain they had endured, and would endure. Tears of anger for their endless battles. Tears of fear for what life might look like. Tears of fatigue. All of these tears and emotions came out all at once. This gift didn't mean they wouldn't still have to fight. But it meant they would be able to fight.

Mike was still in shock. The only thing he could do was get in his pick-up truck and drive to his friend's house. He grabbed his keys and headed out. Thirty minutes later, he knocked on Jason's front door. Jason was faced with a man bawling his eyes out.

Not a word. Mike lunged forward and grabbed Jason. Was it a hug or was he holding on for dear life? It said everything he needed to say. They both knew this would be a long journey, but Mike wouldn't be alone.

Finally, Mike found some words.

"Thank you."

Jason pulled away to look his friend in the face.

"You're welcome."

It was the beginning of another chapter for Mike, a chapter he and his family are still enduring. The cancer treatments continue, and the family carries on. Mike's wife is strong—stronger than most. We pray and hope for a healthy, rejuvenated body for her.

Fly fishing is wonderful in itself, but the friends we fish with, now there's the real wonder. I have faced my own hard times, and my own fishy friends have stepped up in their own ways and said, "Ryan, I got you." From the bottom of my heart, thank you. Thank you for all the years of support and friendship. My life is better with you in it. Cheers to more days on the water, incredible friendships, and chasing fish.

CHECK OUT RYAN JOHNSTON'S OTHER GREAT BOOK

A REEL JOB

SHORT STORIES & THOUGHTS FROM THE RIVER

RYAN JOHNSTON

COVER ARTWORK

DEYOUNG

www.derekdeyoung.com

BOOK LAYOUT & DESIGN

CREATIVE DESIGNS
annaburrous

annaburrous.com

Made in United States
North Haven, CT
09 April 2024

51079563R00119